WITHDRAWN
No longer the property of the
Boston Public Library.
Sale of this material benefits the Library

WITHDRAWN
No longer the property of the
Boston Public Library.
Sale of this material benefits the Library

tweed

Nancy J. Thomas

tweed

MORE THAN 20 CONTEMPORARY DESIGNS TO KNIT

Photography by Jack Deutsch

POTTER
CRAFT

NEW YORK

Copyright © 2008 by Nancy Thomas

All rights reserved.

Published in the United States by Potter Craft, an imprint of the Crown Publishing Group,
a division of Random House, Inc., New York.
www.crownpublishing.com
www.pottercraft.com

POTTER CRAFT and colophon and POTTER and colophon
are registered trademarks of Random House, Inc.

Library of Congress Cataloging-in-Publication Data
Thomas, Nancy J.
Tweed : 20 contemporary designs to knit / Nancy J. Thomas.
p. cm.
Includes index.
ISBN 978-0-307-38132-3
1. Knitting—Patterns. 2. Tweed. I. Title.
TT825.T4445 2007
746.43'2041—dc22   2007029388

Printed in China

Photography by Jack Deutsch
Design by woolypear

Black-and-white historical photographs courtesy of Harris Tweed.

10 9 8 7 6 5 4 3 2 1

First Edition

*For my Grandmother Jessie—for her Scottish heritage
and for teaching me to knit*

ACKNOWLEDGMENTS

I am indebted to many people who made this book possible. I especially want to acknowledge Dee Neer, who wrote every pattern, created all the charts and schematics, and guided me tirelessly through this project. Without her, this book never would have been completed.

I was especially fortunate to receive much sage advice from Francis Walsh of Kilcar, Ireland, about tweed and the development of the yarn industry in the West Coast of Ireland. He was a fountain of knowledge and experience. His yarn and spinning background as well as his historical knowledge proved invaluable.

Diane Friedman was so instrumental in getting the book off the ground and sharing her knowledge of tweed yarns and the woolen spun system. Over thirty years ago, Diane worked with an Irish yarn mill to turn a tightly spun, tweed weaving yarn into a soft, voluminous knitting yarn. I also thank Stacy Charles, who, with the Potter Craft editors, spun my idea into a reality.

For incorporating my vision of an Irish and Scottish landscape in the photos, I'm grateful to have yet again collaborated with photographer Jack Deutsch. He made every photo look beautiful!

I also want to thank the designers and knitters who created the beautiful projects in the book—Linda Cyr, Gitta Schrade, and Jean Frost. They took simple yarn and made fabulous, contemporary projects. The wonderful IDI group—Poonam Thakur, Raj Kachroo, and Indra Dhar—made a big difference. I also thank my knitting friend Maggie McManus for her help.

My great models, Christine Boutte and William Madera, made the tweed projects come alive.

CONTENTS

INTRODUCTION

Why write a book on tweed yarns? As I approached this project, I kept asking myself this question. I grew up knitting with simple, worsted yarns. Who knew that there was a world full of rustic tweed yarn? These wool yarns entered my life in the early 1980s, during my tenure at *Vogue Knitting*. I was accustomed to sleek, modern yarns, but the textures and color infusions of tweed suited my interest in vintage, antique looks. In 1986, *Vogue Knitting* featured a pullover sweater made in Donegal Tweed with a stylized cat on the front. Even though the sweater would be oversized and outdated by today's tastes, that pullover remains one of my favorites. The tweed yarn was a big part of the appeal of the simple, intarsia pullover. Tweed yarn was a new and exciting knitting prospect that I quickly embraced.

My interest in tweed reached a completely new level when, in the mid-1980s and 1990s, I took Fair Isle and Aran knitting classes with author Alice Starmore, who hails from the Outer Hebrides. She was an inspiration to me, meshing the historical foundations of knitting styles and techniques with current trends. Soon, I couldn't get enough of books on the knitting history of the United Kingdom, particularly that of Ireland and Scotland. Authors such as Sheila MacGregor, Rae Compton, and Michael Pearson spun fascinating tales and brought a tapestry of vintage photographs of people and sweaters from the four corners of the British Isles.

In 1995, I traveled to the Shetland Islands to film a video with Alice Starmore and, at the same time, to photograph designs for the Fall 1994 issue of *Vogue Knitting.* I was smitten with the people, the windswept landscape, the sheep and ponies, and, most of all, the history. I found people who loved their knitting and what it represented. These knitters wanted to talk about their heritage and were proud to be engaged in an age-old art, even as alternative sources of income, such as off-shore oil businesses, were diminishing the importance of knitting to their local economies.

In writing this book, I've started with the birthplace of tweed yarns to help you understand how yarn intended for weaving "spun off" into yarns that we now use for hand knitting. Chapter 2 explores the process of making tweed yarns. I consider this the most important chapter in the book; it is your yarn tutorial. Chapter 3 focuses on fabrics to make using tweed yarn. To that end, I start with simple stitches and work up to more complicated ones. If you want to make fabrics that look like classic tweeds, this chapter is the place to start. The last four chapters are the project chapters. This section of the book offers a wide range of projects that emphasize the wonderful qualities of tweed yarns. It starts with easy accessories and moves up to the pieces that require more advanced skills. None of the projects in this book is terribly difficult, but each can help build your knitting proficiency.

In *Tweed* I've chosen to explore what is basically a fabric story that turned into a yarn and knitting story. Now, each time you pick up needles to work with a traditional tweed yarn (or a not-so-traditional one), you'll be embarking on an adventure that goes back centuries and you'll be a part of a very special knitting legacy.

Stornoway Harbor, Scotland, home of Harris Tweed.

Chapter 1

ORIGINS OF TWEED YARNS AND FABRICS

To fully appreciate the history of tweed yarns, one must know something about the history of the British Isles. The struggle to move from a land of hunters, farmers, and fishers to an industrialized nation brought sweeping changes throughout the land. Some events, such as the discovery that sheep's wool could be turned into yarn, were pure accidents, whereas the development of woven fabrics was more an evolution. This historical chapter will not talk much about knitting. The formation of tweed yarn and fabrics is a story about woven fabric, not knit fabric.

The story of tweed begins in the pastures with the sheep and extends all the way through the mills, where the yarn is spun. But the story of tweed also concerns a land, a people, and a rich history. It's the story of a transition from spinners with simple drop spindles to machine-spun yarns using age-old technologies, and the difference between high-tech machines that create yarns with perfect regularity but little texture and the older machines that crank out homespun-looking yarn.

One thing is for certain: The tweed yarn we have today came from rustic wool that was used to create even more rustic garments. Over time, fashion has driven changes in the making of tweed yarns. Coco Chanel translated tweed fabrics used in menswear into high-fashion pieces. Colors have evolved in response to contemporary tastes and to reflect the shades found in ready-to-wear. Classic jackets and skirts in classic colors are the mainstay of true tweed makers. Tweed yarns weren't introduced for knitting consumption until the 1970s.

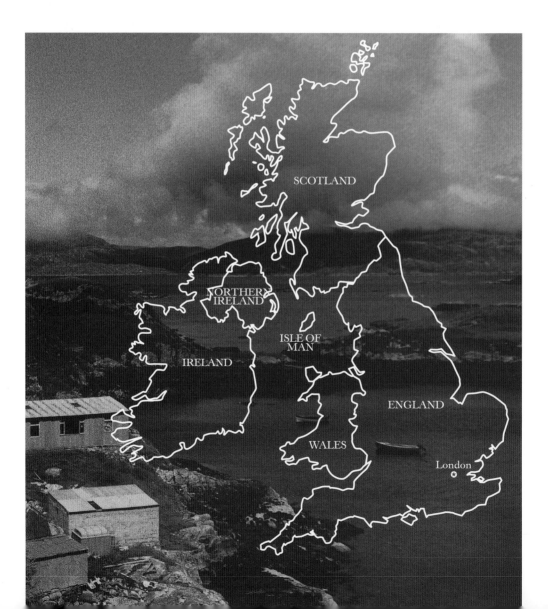

Queen Elizabeth II and Prince Phillip on a visit to Harris Tweed in Stornoway, Scotland.

Will the Real Tweed Please Stand Up?

When I began my research on tweed yarns, I asked Francis Walsh, a yarn spinner from Kilcar in Donegal with twenty-six years of experience, the meaning of *tweed*. His interest in the cultural, social, and economic history of the Western Coastal region of Ireland provided great insight. He explained that initially *tweed* was a term to describe a rough, woolen, handwoven cloth used mainly in menswear in Scotland and Ireland. Already this was starting out to be a curious adventure. Didn't you think of tweed as a yarn with flecks of color interspersed throughout? But the word *tweed* didn't begin with our present-day conception.

Francis went on to say that the word *tweed* may have derived from the Tweed River, a ninety-seven-mile (156km) long river that flows to the North Sea through the Border region of Scotland. The Tweed River is known as one of the great salmon rivers of Scotland, and its lower portion marks the border between Scotland and England. Another popular theory is that the word *tweed* might have been a simple misnomer that came into existence when someone misread the word *tweel*, the original Scottish word for *twill*. Indeed, the Scottish tweeds get the most publicity and are probably the best known. But even though all signs seem to point to Scotland as the birthplace of tweed, I quickly discovered that no one area can claim tweed homespun fabric as its own, because these fabrics were also being spun in Northern Ireland and the Lake District of Britain at about the same time. What we do know for certain, however, is that around the mid- to late 1800s, people in the countryside of England, Scotland, and Northern Ireland (mainly farmers and fishers) looked beyond their own fences and began to unite to make and sell their wares, including tweed fabrics. *Tweed* eventually became the general term used to describe all carded, "homespun" wool, whether it was Scotch tweed, Irish tweed, Donegal tweed, Cheviot tweed, or Harris tweed.

Harris Tweed weaver, Marion Campbell, preparing her loom for weaving.

Fabric Designs

People throughout the United Kingdom were producing tweed, but why did these fabrics all look alike? Look at the map on page 12 and take note of the short distance from Ireland to England and Ireland to Scotland. Even in the early days of the famines of the 1800s workers and crafts-people moved between Scotland and Donegal County, Ireland, in search of work and at the same time exchanging products and ideas.

Originally, the heavier-weight woolen fabrics were made to resist the rainy weather in Ireland and Scotland, but as time went on, lighter-weight woolen fabrics were introduced for indoor wear. In the 1890s, tweed fabrics were made into jackets and long skirts for women and the first tweed "suits" became available. In the 1950s and 1960s, Coco Chanel brought tweed fabrics into the realm of high fashion with her signature suits and jackets.

One of the most famous fabrics is Harris Tweed, a trademarked name dating from the early 1800s. The first owner of Harris was Lady Dunmore, who had the Harris weavers copy tartans, which she then sold to her friends. Authentic Harris Tweed plaids are woven from yarn that is dyed and spun in the Outer Hebrides of Scotland.

If you travel to the British Isles or shop where fine imported goods are sold, you may encounter these tweeds: Magee of Donegal (Ireland), Linton Tweed (Scotland), Anthony Haines (Scotland), Bernat Klein (Scotland), Johnstons of Elgin (Scotland), J C Rennie (Scotland), and Alexanders (Scotland).

Tweed Fabrics

In spite of their similarities, tweed fabrics are distinctive. Here are some of the common names used to describe tweed fabric, both knit and woven.

Cheviot tweed The name comes from a British breed of sheep originating in the Northumber-land region and known for its heavy fleece. Cloth produced from this wool has a heavy twill weave. It is sometimes called Scotch tweed.

Herringbone A pattern consisting of adjoining vertical rows of slanting lines suggesting a V or an inverted V. It is also known as chevron.

Houndstooth check A pattern of broken or jagged checks.

Twill weave One of three basic weave structures in which the filling threads (woof threads) are woven over and under two or more warp yarns, producing the characteristic diagonal pattern.

Worsted Firmly twisted yarn or thread spun from combed, stapled wool fibers of the same length. Cloth produced from this yarn has a hard, smooth surface and no nap (like corduroy or velvet).

THE DONEGAL TWEED STORY

For the best place to find out about Irish tweed (specifically the trademarked Donegal Tweed), you need to travel to the northwestern-most part of the Republic of Ireland, to a county called Donegal, known for its North Atlantic–facing coast, high cliffs, beaches, and windswept peninsulas. *Donegal* is a term that comes from the Irish *Dun na ngall*, meaning "fort of the foreigner."

The inhabitants of Donegal had been spinning yarn for woven fabric for hundreds of years. In the nineteenth century, much of wool production and loomed fabric weaving took place in the home and was not the work of mills or factories. A skilled home weaver could weave about 30 yards (27 meters) a day, which was sold to a distribution point or directly at local markets. But in 1890 the craft grew into a local industry. That was the year when Sir Arthur Balfour, the chief secretary of Ireland, visited some of Ireland's most depressed regions, and in response to the poverty he witnessed, passed the Purchase of Land Act, which would forever change the fortunes of the people in the region. This act established what were called the Congested District Boards, which set new standards for spinning and weaving in addition to fishing, agriculture, forestry, and livestock breeding. As a result of this initiative, new breeds of sheep and less-inbred sheep were raised, which, in turn, created higher-quality wool. But the boards also set more stringent guidelines for wool production.

Before the advent of the Congested District Boards, oftentimes lesser-grade wool was not carded or combed properly, and dirt and twigs would remain in the wool. To compound the problem, the weavers, in an attempt to maximize their production, would hastily prepare fabric. After the boards were established, an inspection site was set up in Ardara to grade the finished products. The weavers received wages and bonuses based on the quality, not the quantity, of the fabric they produced. Soon Donegal Tweed gained a reputation as a superior, highly sought-after product.

Today the main factory for Donegal Tweed fabric is Magee, Molloy & McNutt, which produces more than 600 yards (550 meters) in a day. This industrialized company still employs some local craftspeople to weave traditional Donegal Tweed fabrics.

Since the 1970s, the mill at Kilcar has made yarn for export, including tweed yarns like those used for the projects in this book.

Queen Elizabeth II observes the tweed-making process.

Chapter 2

IT ALL STARTS WITH THE WOOL

The process of making tweed yarn begins with the fiber harvested from a sheep's coat and culminates with the addition of nepps or burrs, the flecks that give tweed its distinctive look. Not all modern tweeds are 100 percent wool, but for the purposes of this book and our technical discussion, we will continue to refer to tweed yarn as all wool. This chapter provides an overview of how woolen-spun tweeds differ from other types of yarn, notably those made under the worsted system. Once you know something about how the yarn is made, I will help you get your knitting needles started with some basic information on yarn weights, what kind of balls to look for, and, most important, suggestions on how to care for finished projects made in tweed wool yarns.

Why Is Sheep's Wool So Good?

Let's start where it all begins: with the sheep themselves. The fibers on a sheep's outer coat that eventually turn into wool are different from the hair or fur of other animals, in that the fibers have what are called scales and crimp. Scales and crimp work together to create both good and bad qualities in wool. Because they attach themselves to neighboring fibers, they make it easy to spin wool into yarn. This property also means that wool requires special care if you don't want to unintentionally felt your finished sweater. Tweed yarns are especially prone to felting because of their makeup (more on that later, when we discuss how to care for wool).

So let's talk about crimp in a wool fiber. Crimp gives wool its ability to keep you dry by absorbing moisture (called wicking), which makes it ideal for staying warm (or cool if you happen to be wearing a wool garment in the desert). The amount of crimp in a fiber relates to the fineness of the wool. Fine wool from Merino sheep may have up to a hundred crimps per inch (2.5cm). Coarse wools may have only a few crimps per inch (2.5cm). Generally, fiber manufacturers don't tell you how many crimps your wool has. They use descriptive words and phrases, such as *extra fine Merino* or *fine, soft wool*. Sometimes wool is discussed in terms of micrometers to measure the fiber diameter of wool. In this method of measuring, the coarser the wool, the higher the micrometer count. Tweed yarns are less fine than fine, soft merinos.

The Process of Turning Wool into Yarn

Spinners begin with the fleece freshly obtained from the sheared sheep. These bunches of fleece are not pretty. In fact, they are quite dirty and may even have pieces of brush and other plant matter embedded in them. Since a sheep's coat is also full of grease, or lanolin, the first step is to wash the coat and get rid of the grease, dirt, and other impurities. Once the fleeces are cleaned, they are graded. Not all the graded wool is turned into knitting yarn. These days a great deal of commercial wool is diverted to become carpeting, rugs, upholstery, and even felt to insulate machinery.

Carding

After they're clean, the wool fibers go through several more steps before becoming yarn. The first step is known as *carding*. When hand-spinners are carding wool, they use handheld devices to line up and refine the fibers in preparation for spinning. During the machine carding process, machines draw the fibers through several rollers, organizing and preparing them to be spun into a roving yarn or to move onto additional steps.

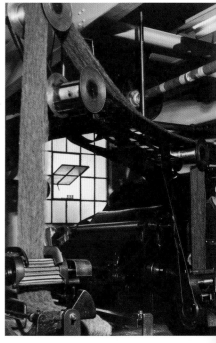

Wool coming off the carding machine at the Harris Tweed mill.

Two Systems

Many of the yarns we buy today are created using a worsted system, but traditional wool tweeds are made using the woolen system. Very few yarns, aside from tweed, are produced using the woolen system. Here are the major differences between the two systems.

**The top yarn is made using the woolen system,
and the bottom yarn is created with the worsted system.**

WOOLEN SPINNING SYSTEM

» *Processes rustic and simple yarns. Wool fibers are carded up to seven times during the process.*

» *Involves several stages but no combing.*

» *The fibers go directly from carding to the spinning process.*

» *Wool fibers used for woolen spinning are short (and, thus, better for felting).*

» *The fibers are not parallel but cross in different directions, making a more textured finished yarn.*

» *The end product is uneven and can be pulled apart easily for a rustic look and feel. The twist is looser and less refined.*

WORSTED SPINNING SYSTEM

» *More complex process involving opening, blending, cleaning, and carding, followed by combing, drawing, and spinning.*

» *The wool used is medium or longer in length. Fiber lengths vary from 2" to 7" (5cm to 18cm).*

» *The fibers are in a parallel formation to create a smoother finished product.*

» *The resulting yarns are compact, smooth, and more even. The end product is stronger than yarns spun using the woolen system.*

Tweed nepps are small flecks of felted fiber that began as an accident but have become the most defining characteristic of tweed yarns.

Technical Terms

Here are a few helpful terms to know when talking about rustic wool yarns.

Carding Preparatory process of getting the fibers ready for spinning.

Nepp A small fiber bit added to yarn in the final spinning process to create tweed effects; sometimes called a *burr* or a *fleck*.

Micron Measure used to describe the fineness of wool.

Ply or plies A strand or strands of yarn used alone or joined with other strands to make a yarn. A ply is not necessarily thin and should not be confused with the ultimate yarn weight. For example, a bulky-weight yarn could be a simple one-ply yarn, and a three- or four-ply yarn could be a fine, lace-weight yarn.

Single-spun yarn One ply of yarn. Single plies are twisted together in opposite directions to make a multi-plied yarn.

Spinning Process used to create yarn.

Warp In weaving, the vertical threads of a loom used in weaving.

Weft In weaving, the horizontal threads inserted by a shuttle through warp threads to make fabric.

Woolen system Yarn-making method that produces a more homespun look.

Worsted system Refined yarn-making method used to spin wool into yarn.

From top to bottom: a skein or hank; a doughnut ball; and an elongated ball, sometimes also called a skein.

Yarn wound by ball winder (top); hand-wound (bottom).

Care and Feeding of Tweed Yarns

Most traditional yarns, including wool tweeds, are wound into skeins or hanks rather than balls. European yarn commonly has some standard weights. For example, the 1¾-ounce (50-gram) ball generally will have come from a European mill. A skein of 100 grams equals 3½ ounces and is a frequently used weight for tweed yarns.

If you buy yarn in skeins, you'll need to turn your skein into a ball. This can be done with a ball winder or by hand-winding a ball. Begin by carefully untwisting the skein. Skeins usually are tied in one or two places. One of the ties will be the beginning and ending strands of yarn. Use a yarn swift to hold the yarn skein while you wind it by hand or try a ball winder. If you don't have a swift, you can place the yarn over a chair or have a helper hold the yarn in his or her arms while you wind the ball. Take care not to wind the ball too tightly because that will compress the yarn.

It is always safest to wash wool garments by hand. I recommend using a mild soap in cool water, and be sure to avoid highly agitating the fabric. It's OK to bend some of these rules, depending on the type of wool you're using. Some wools felt very easily, and some don't. If you have doubts, wash a swatch first and see what happens. Some of the newer "no rinse" wool washes can be used in the washing machine. I've gotten good results when I've filled the washing machine with cold water and then added wool wash followed by my sweaters. After allowing the sweaters to soak and clean, use the delicate spin cycle to remove the water. Lie the sweaters flat to dry.

Whole books have been written on the best blocking and drying methods. Choose your favorite. Where you live and the equipment you have on hand will dictate how you dry your sweaters, throws, and other knit items. If you don't have much space, you can modify your blocking by allowing your piece to dry on a towel on the floor for a few hours and then moving it off the floor and onto a rack.

FELTING

For many of us, our first time felting (sometimes called "fulling") occurred when we accidentally slipped a wool sweater into the washing machine. More than likely, the result was almost always a miniature version of your favorite sweater. (I once felted a beautiful Shetland shawl in just such a mix-up, and I now use it as a table cover.)

The amount of shrinkage for felting depends on several factors: the heat of the water, how much agitation is involved, and what kind of detergent is used. Hot water, great agitation, and strong detergent make the felting work better. Tweed yarns have more dimension when felted. Often the tweed flecks "pop" to the surface, creating a textural fabric.

HOW TO FELT

» Set the washing machine for a hot wash and a cold rinse. The alternating of hot and cold shocks the fibers, producing quicker felting.

» Place the piece in a pillowcase, and baste the case shut to keep the fibers from clogging the washing machine. You can also use a zippered lingerie bag.

» Set the water level at low; use the hottest possible water.

» Place the pillowcase or bag in the washer with a small amount of detergent and an old towel, a pair of old jeans, or a few rubber balls to help the felting process. Set the washer for maximum agitation.

» It's a good idea to check the wash every few minutes. Remember: you can always felt more, but if something is felted too much, it cannot be undone.

» After about ten to fifteen minutes, run the machine through the rinse cycle on cold rinse.

» If your piece requires more felting, repeat the hot and cold cycles as necessary. You want to felt the fabric until you can barely see any stitching and the piece looks more like fabric than knitting.

» Carefully spin the piece dry, using a gentle cycle. You might want to omit this step, especially with large pieces, as the spinning might create difficult-to-remove creases.

» Lay the piece flat on a sweater-drying rack or on towels. The finished size of your piece will be determined by the amount of felting or the shaping done after the piece(s) are removed from the washer (or both).

» Drying time varies, depending on the thickness of the fabric and the humidity level in the air. Sometimes it may take a day or two to dry completely.

Tweed yarn wound from skeins.

Chapter 3

MAKING IT WITH TWEED

Now it's time to turn tweed yarn into knitted fabric. The difference between woven fabric and knit fabric is that woven fabric is worked with two perpendicular strands, known as a *warp* and a *weft*. Knitting is achieved with a continuous strand of yarn. When knitting with a tweed yarn, the first thing you'll probably notice is its rustic texture. But the other element to consider is the contrasting tones of the nepps, which add a vibrant touch of color whether you're working on one or more colors. As you knit, you'll notice how beautifully you can see stitch patterns, especially cables.

The Gaelic Hat can be found on page 52.

When you first begin knitting with tweed, start out with swatches and then try incorporating them into projects. Make a scarf or a sweater. Pillows are easy, serving as unshaped canvases for your knitting art. Begin with a simple one-color knit-and-purl pattern and move to more involved stitches. Simple stitches and cables and bobbles work best for casual pieces. And don't limit your thinking to sweaters—consider accessories and home décor pieces as well. Mix and match patterns within the same piece, but make sure that your gauges are similar to keep your fabric the same width.

I've included a range of patterns to showcase tweed yarns, beginning with the simplest knit and purl stitches. The next range of patterns with cables shows how wonderfully tweeds work for textural patterning. The last few patterns in this section simulate tweed fabrics. Look at a good stitch dictionary for additional two-color slip stitch patterns. These patterns are the ultimate tweeds and can add a new dimension to knitted tweed fabrics. By working with two or more colors in a slip stitch pattern, you are creating a woven appearance not found in other knitting patterns. One or two little changes in stitch or color completely change the result. If you took the Pearl Tweed fabric on page 35 and changed the more natural yellow shade to a lively purple contrasting color, you would have a completely different swatch. Have fun and enjoy your tweed experimentation!

Creating Tweed Fabric Looks in Knitting

Many tweed yarns give fantastic stitch definition. The nepps or flecks add interest without detracting from the stitches themselves. For the tweed yarns discussed here, you will be working with 100 percent wool or with yarns of a high wool content. Wool is a truly "forgiving" fiber. But even if you don't have the neatest tension, not to worry. Steam or block your swatch, and all the unevenness will be removed.

Where to start if this is your first time knitting with tweed yarn? My best advice is to begin with simple knit and purl stitches in one color. As you advance, you can work up to cables, bobbles, and two-color fabrics. You may not be up to designing your own projects, but stitch patterns can be a jumping-off point. Use the stitches as simple rectangles, and use a stitch pattern to make a scarf, pillow, or bag. When incorporating patterns into your own project, it is most important to understand how to work with multiples. Let's use the Ribbons pattern (page 29) as an example. This stitch requires a multiple of six stitches plus three extra stitches. Consider using three multiples of the pattern. This would require you to cast on twenty-one stitches: eighteen stitches (three multiples) plus three extra stitches (added once). Once you know how to handle multiples, you can easily adapt and substitute patterns.

Tips on Stitch Patterns in Tweeds

Make your swatches large enough to really see the stitch patterns. Don't worry about all that extra knitting time. You can turn your swatches into a pillow or an interesting bag. You can also felt them and cut them up to use as appliqués.

» *Try a few different needle sizes if you are unsure of what size is suitable for your yarn weight. Generally, you want a flexible fabric, not too stiff and not too loose. Most tweed yarns benefit from a looser gauge. Trial and error will help you see what works best.*

» *To use your swatch to measure a gauge, it's easier if you add edge stitches and rows. You can also add two or three stitches at each end of the swatch and knit them on every row. Usually two or three rows in garter stitch after the cast-on and before the bind-off rows will help. If you want to define the stitches further, place markers around your pattern stitch.*

» *Choose lighter colors for the most intricate stitches. Dark shades make it more difficult to see beautiful cabling and the contrast between knit and purl stitches.*

» *When working two-color patterns, combine some unexpected color palettes.*

» *Keep going. Your pattern may not be obvious after only a couple of rows. To get the full effect, work several row repeats.*

» *Tack up your swatch. Stand back and look at it for the full effect. Does it do what you expected it to do? Do you need to change colors or stitches?*

» *Your swatch may require a little finishing. Steam or spray it, pin to size, and let it dry.*

NEPPS, FLECKS, or BURRS

I turned to expert Francis Walsh to find out about the origin of tweed flecks. From him I learned that the addition of *nepps* to tweed fabric was a fortunate accident that occurred around the time that wool spinners began using several shades of wool during the carding process. Instead of having one monotone shade, the spinners were able to produce yarns with shade variations and depth—some even with low-contrast flecks. Occasionally, a bit of yarn would not get completely integrated into the fiber and, when spun, turned into a large fleck.

At some point, spinners began to deliberately add small pinches of felted bits in a contrasting color to the final carding. Whereas normal unfelted fibers would be drawn into the spinning to change the shade of the yarn, the felted nepps stayed intact. This look really caught on and special machinery was introduced to accommodate the tweed nepp, thereby enabling spinners to mass produce tweed yarns.

One other special tidbit Francis shared with me is that in the Southwest Donegal area the process of adding nepps is different from anywhere else. He told me that while most, if not all, carding techniques outside Donegal apply the fleck at the final stage of carding, in Donegal tweed the fleck is mixed with the rest of the fiber before the first stage of carding. The result is a fleck that is better integrated into the yarn and does not shed when woven or knit.

COLORS OF THE FIRST DONEGAL TWEED YARNS AND NEPPS

Before the use of natural dyes, wool colors came only from the color of the sheep. Of course, there were the traditional off-white, black, and brown shades. Various blends of these colors could be made by mixing off-white and black for shades of gray and off-white and brown to create taupe and light brown.

To add more color to the nepps, the locals turned to the colors found in the natural landscape of Ireland. They looked at earth- and rock-colored browns, at gold from sheaves of wheat, at green from the pastures, and at the blues of slate stones and the sky. To simulate natural hues, they gathered yellows from local flowers called Gorse, reds and purples from berries, greens from moss, and oranges from lichen. The colors that originated with Donegal tweed are still incorporated into modern tweed fabrics.

Knit and Purl Stitches

The following stitch patterns are relatively easy, and they all have less than twenty-row repeats. Some have as few two rows.

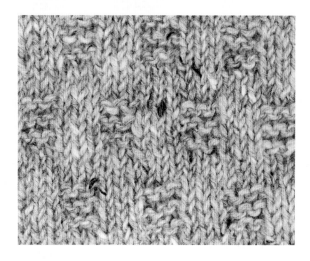

Simple Basket Weave (multiple of 8 stitches)

Row 1 (right side) Knit.

Rows 2–6 *K4, p4; repeat from * to end.

Row 7 Knit.

Rows 8–12 *P4, k4; repeat from * to end.

Repeat rows 1–12 for simple basket weave.

Ribbons (multiple of 6 stitches + 3 extra stitches)

Rows 1, 3, and 5 (right side) *P3, k3; repeat from * across, end p3.

Rows 2, 4, 6, and 8 Purl.

Rows 7 and 9 Knit.

Rows 10, 12, and 14 *P3, k3; repeat from * across, end p3.

Rows 11, 13, 15, and 17 Knit.

Rows 16 and 18 Purl.

Repeat rows 1–18 for ribbons.

SIMPLE BASKET WEAVE

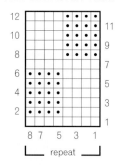

☐ Knit on right side, purl on wrong side

⊡ Purl on right side, knit on wrong side

RIBBONS

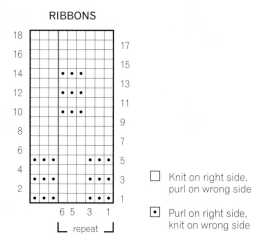

☐ Knit on right side, purl on wrong side

⊡ Purl on right side, knit on wrong side

Easy Ribbing

(multiple of 2 stitches + 1 extra stitch)

Row 1 (right side) *K1, p1; repeat from * across to the last stitch, end k1.

Row 2 Purl.

Repeat rows 1 and 2 for easy ribbing.

EASY
RIBBING

☐ Knit on right side,
purl on wrong side

● Purl on right side,
knit on wrong side

Garter Ridge Ribbing (multiple of 3 stitches)

Rows 1 and 3 (right side) K1, *p1, k2; repeat from * across to the last 2 stitches, end p1, k1.

Row 2 K2, *p2, k1; repeat from * across to the last stitch, end k1.

Row 4 Knit.

Repeat rows 1–4 for garter ridge ribbing.

GARTER RIDGE
RIBBING

☐ Knit on right side,
purl on wrong side

● Purl on right side,
knit on wrong side

Seed Rib Checks

(multiple of 4 stitches + 3 extra stitches)

Note: The stitch pattern looks the same on both the right side and the wrong side.

Row 1 K3, *p1, k3; repeat from * to end.

Row 2 K1, *p1, k3; repeat from * across to the last 2 stitches, end p1, k1.

Rows 3 and 5 Repeat row 1.

Rows 4 and 6 Repeat row 2.

Rows 7, 9, and 11 Repeat row 2.

Rows 8, 10, and 12 Repeat row 1.

Repeat rows 1–12 for seed rib checks.

SEED RIB CHECKS

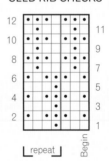

☐ Knit on right side,
purl on wrong side

● Purl on right side,
knit on wrong side

Cables

All these cable patterns spell out the cabling at the beginning of the pattern.

Hill Cables

(multiple of 12 stitches + 6 extra stitches)

C6B (6-stitch right cable) Slip 3 stitches onto a cable needle and hold to the back, knit 3 stitches, knit 3 stitches from the cable needle.

Rows 1, 3, and 5 (right side) *K6, p6; repeat from * across, end k6.

Row 2 and all wrong-side rows Purl.

Row 7 *C6B, p6; repeat from * across, end C6B.

Rows 9, 11, and 13 *P6, k6; repeat from * across, end p6.

Row 15 *P6, C6B; repeat from * across, end p6.

Row 16 Purl.

Repeat rows 1–16 for hill cables.

HILL CABLES

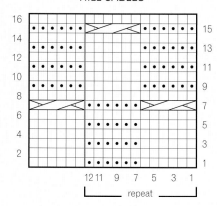

12 11 9 7 5 3 1

└── repeat ──┘

☐ Knit on right side, purl on wrong side

• Purl on right side, knit on wrong side

  C6B

Cable Knots

(multiple of 12 stitches + 3 extra stitches)

C6B (6-stitch right cable) Slip 3 stitches onto a cable needle and hold to the back, knit 3 stitches, knit 3 stitches from the cable needle.

C6F (6-stitch left cable) Slip 3 stitches onto a cable needle and hold to the front, knit 3 stitches, knit 3 stitches from the cable needle.

k1-tbl (knit 1 through the back loop)

p1-tbl (purl 1 through the back loop)

Row 1 (right side) *P1, k1-tbl, p1, k9; repeat from * across to the last 3 stitches, end p1, k1-tbl , p1.

Row 2 and all wrong-side rows *K1, p1-tbl, k1, p9; repeat from * across to the last 3 stitches, end k1, p1-tbl, k1.

Row 3 *P1, k1-tbl, p1, k3, C6F; repeat from * across to the last 3 stitches, end p1, k1-tbl, p1.

Row 5 Repeat row 1.

Row 7 *P1, k1-tbl, p1, C6B, k3; repeat from * across to the last 3 stitches, end p1, k1-tbl, p1.

Row 8 Repeat row 2.

Repeat rows 1–8 for cable knots pattern.

CABLE KNOTS

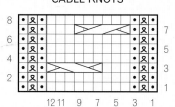

12 11 9 7 5 3 1

☐ Knit on right side, purl on wrong side

• Purl on right side, knit on wrong side

Ⓧ K1-tbl on right side, p1-tbl on wrong side

▭ C6B

▭ C6F

Combo of Stitches

This beautiful fabric combines cables, leaves, and bobbles. It's a challenge that's well worth the effort.

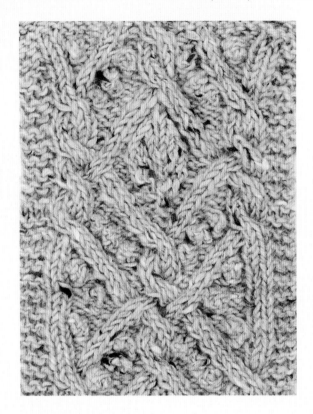

Diamond Leaf Cable

(panel of 25 stitches)

C3pB (3-stitch right cable) Slip 1 stitch onto a cable needle and hold to the back, knit 2 stitches, purl 1 stitch from the cable needle.

C3pF (3-stitch left cable) Slip 2 stitches onto a cable needle and hold to the front, purl 1 stitch, knit 2 stitches from the cable needle.

C5Bp (5-stitch right cable) Slip 3 stitches onto a cable needle and hold to the back, knit 2 stitches, then purl 1 stitch, knit 2 stitches from the cable needle.

C5Fp (5-stitch left cable) Slip 2 stitches onto a cable needle and hold to the front, knit 2 stitches, purl 1 stitch, then knit 2 stitches from the cable needle.

dcd (double centered decrease) Slip 2 stitches together knitwise to the right-hand needle, knit 1 stitch, pass the 2 slipped stitches over the knit stitch.

M1 (make 1) An increase that is made by lifting the strand between the needles to the left-hand needle and knitting the strand through the back loop, twisting it to prevent a hole.

MB (make bobble) (right side) Knit into the front loop, the back loop, then the front loop of the next stitch (make 3 stitches in 1); turn, purl 3 stitches; turn, knit 3 stitches together—1 stitch remains.

Note: The leaf insert begins at row 15 and is noted in angled brackets (< >).

Row 1 (right side) K2, p2, MB, p2, C5Bp, p1, C5Bp, p2, MB, p2, k2.

Row 2 and all wrong-side rows Knit the knit stitches and purl the purl stitches as they face you; also purl the remaining bobble stitch and the remaining stitch from the leaf insert, when present from the previous row.

Row 3 K2, p4, C3pB, p1, C5Fp, p1, C3pF, p4, k2.

Row 5 K2, p1, MB, p1, C3pB, p2, k2, p1, k2, p2, C3pF, p1, MB, p1, k2.

Row 7 K2, p2, C3pB, p1, MB, p1, k2, p1, k2, p1, MB, p1, C3pF, p2, k2.

Row 9 K2, p1, C3pB, p1, MB, p2, C5Fp, p2, MB, p1, C3pF, p1, k2.

Row 11 C5Fp, p1, MB, p2, C3pB, p1, C3pF, p2, MB, p1, C5Fp.

Row 13 K2, p1, k2, p3, C3pB, p1, k1-tbl, p1, C3pF, p3, k2, p1, k2.

Row 15 K2, p1, k2, p2, C3pB, p2, <M1, k1-tbl, M1>, p2, C3pF, p2, k2, p1, k2.

Row 17 C5Fp, p1, C3pB, p3, <k1, yo, k1-tbl, yo, k1>, p3, C3pF, p1, C5Fp.

Row 19 K2, p1, C5Bp, p4, <k2, yo, k1-tbl, yo, k2>, p4, C5Bp, p1, k2.

Row 21 C5Fp, p1, C3pF, p3, <ssk, k3, k2tog>, p3, C3pB, p1, C5Fp.

Row 23 K2, p1, k2, p2, C3pF, p2, <ssk, k1, k2tog>, p2, C3pB, p2, k2, p1, k2.

Row 25 K2, p1, k2, p3, C3pF, p1, <dcd>, p1, C3pB, p3, k2, p1, k2.

Row 27 C5Fp, p1, MB, p2, C3pF, p1, C3pB, p2, MB, p1, C5Fp.

Row 29 K2, p1, C3pF, p1, MB, p2, C5Fp, p2, MB, p1, C3pB, p1, k2.

Row 31 K2, p2, C3pF, p1, MB, p1, k2, p1, k2, p1, MB, p1, C3pB, p2, k2.

Row 33 K2, p1, MB, p1, C3pF, p2, k2, p1, k2, p2, C3pB, p1, MB, p1, k2.

Row 35 K2, p4, C3pF, p1, C5Fp, p1, C3pB, p4, k2.

Row 36 Repeat row 2.

Repeat rows 1–36 for diamond leaf cable.

DIAMOND LEAF CABLE PANEL

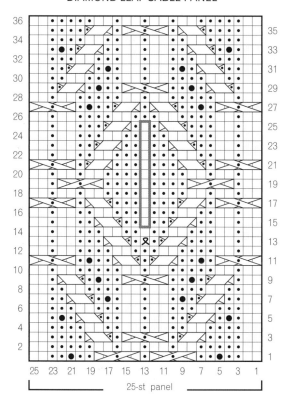

25-st panel

	Knit on right side, purl on wrong side		C3pB
•	Purl on right side, knit on wrong side		C3pF
●	MB		C5Bp
⊠	K1-tbl		C5Fp

LEAF INSERT
(Diamond Leaf Cable)

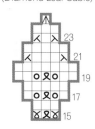

⊠	M1
⊠	K1-tbl
⊡	Yo
⊼	K2tog
⊠	Ssk
⋀	Dcd

TWEED FABRIC

Use these stitches to simulate tweed woven fabrics. Most are simple slip stitches that require working with only one color in each row.

Twill

(multiple of 9 stitches + 1 extra stitch)

M1 (make 1) An increase that is made by lifting the strand between the needles to the left-hand needle and knitting the strand through the back loop, twisting it to prevent a hole.

Row 1 (wrong side) Purl.

Row 2 (right side) *K2tog, k3, M1, k4; repeat from * across to the last stitch, end k1.

Row 3 Purl.

Row 4 K4, *M1, k4, k2tog, k3; repeat from * across, end M1, k4, k2tog.

Repeat rows 1–4 for twill.

TWILL STITCH

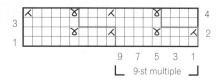

9-st multiple

	Knit on right side, purl on wrong side
⊠	M1
⊼	K2tog

Birdy Tweed

(multiple of 6 stitches + 3 extra stitches)

Note: This design was originally featured in Barbara Walker's Second Treasury of Knitting Patterns *as "Butterfly Quilting."*

Color A is the main color, and color B is the contrasting color.

Slip all stitches purlwise, with the float (the strand of yarn crossing over the slipped stitches) held to the right side of the fabric on both the right-side rows (held in front of the stitches while slipping them) and the wrong-side rows (held in back of the stitches while slipping them). When slipping the multiple stitches (rows 1, 2, 7, and 8), be sure that the yarn is stranded very loosely across the right side of the fabric.

Cast on with color A.

Foundation Row (wrong side) Purl 1 row.
Row 1 (right side) With B, k2, *slip 5 stitches *with yarn in front*, k1; repeat from * across to the last stitch, k1.
Row 2 With B, p2, *slip 5 stitches *with yarn in back*, p1; repeat from * across to the last stitch, p1.
Row 3 With A, knit.
Row 4 With A, purl.
Row 5 With A, k4, *insert the left-hand needle under the 2 floats (loose B strands) and knit the next stitch under the 2 strands, allowing the strands to fall in back of the stitch (tack stitch), k5; repeat from * across, end last repeat k4 instead of k5.
Row 6 With A, purl.
Row 7 With B, k1, slip 3 *with yarn in front*, *k1, slip 5 stitches *with yarn in front*; repeat from * across to the last 5 stitches, end k1, slip 3 *with yarn in front*, k1.

Row 8 With B, p1, slip 3 *with yarn in back*, *p1, slip 5 stitches *with yarn in back*; repeat from * across to the last 5 stitches, end p1, slip 3 stitches *with yarn in back*, p1.
Rows 9 and 10 With A, repeat rows 3 and 4.
Row 11 With A, k1, *insert the left-hand needle under the 2 floats and knit the next stitch under the 2 strands, allowing the strands to fall in back of the stitch (tack stitch), k5; repeat from * across to last 2 stitches, end tack stitch, k1.
Row 12 With A, purl.
Repeat rows 1–12 for birdy tweed.

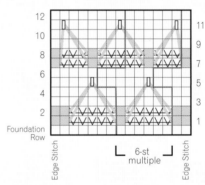

BIRDY TWEED

☐ With A, purl on wrong side, knit on right side

▨ With B, knit or purl

⩔⩔⩔⩔⩔ Slip 5 stitches

⩔⩔⩔ Slip 3 stitches

Ⅱ Tack stitch (see row 5 or 11)

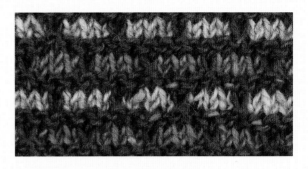

Pearl Tweed (multiple of 3 stitches + 2 extra stitches)

Note: Color A is the main color, and color B is the contrasting color. For a foundation, cast on with the main color and work 2 rows in stockinette stitch.

Row 1 (right side) With B, k1, *slip 2 *with yarn in front*, k1; repeat from *, end k1.

Row 2 With B, p1, *k1, p1, slip 1 *with yarn in front*; repeat from *, end p1.

Row 3 With A, k3, *slip 1 *with yarn in back*, k2; repeat from *, end slip 1 *with yarn in back*, k1.

Row 4 With A, purl.

Row 5 With B, k2, *slip 2 *with yarn in front*, k1; repeat from * to end.

Row 6 With B, p2, *slip 1 *with yarn in front*, k1, p1; repeat from * to end.

Row 7 With A, k1, *slip 1 *with yarn in back*, k2; repeat from *, end k1.

Row 8 With A, purl.

Row 9 With B, k1, slip 1 *with yarn in front*, *k1, slip 2 with yarn in front; repeat from *, end k1, slip 1 *with yarn in front*, k1.

Row 10 With B, p1, *slip 1 *with yarn in front*, k1, p1; repeat from *, end p1.

Row 11 With A, k2, *slip 1 *with yarn in back*, k2; repeat from * to end.

Row 12 With A, purl.

Repeat rows 1–12 for pearl tweed.

Slip Stitch Masonry Pattern
(multiple of 4 stitches + 3 extra stitches)

Note: Color A is the main color, and colors B and C are the contrasting colors.

Rows 1 and 2 With A, knit.

Row 3 (right side) With B, k1, *slip 1 stitch *with yarn in back*, k3; repeat from *, end slip 1 with *yarn in back*, k1.

Row 4 With B, p1, slip 1 *with yarn in front*, *p3, slip 1 *with yarn in front*; repeat from *, end p1.

Rows 5 and 6 With A, knit.

Row 7 With C, k1, *k2, slip 1 *with yarn in back*, k1; repeat from *, end k2.

Row 8 With C, p2, *p1, slip 1 *with yarn in front* (right side of fabric), p2; repeat from *, end p1.

Repeat rows 1–8 for slip stitch masonry pattern.

SLIP STITCH MASONRY

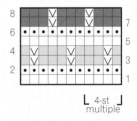

L 4-st J
multiple

☐ Knit on right side, purl on wrong side

• Purl on right side, knit on wrong side

▨ With B, knit or purl

▨ With C, knit or purl

Ⅴ Slip 1 with yarn in back on right side, with yarn in front on wrong side

PEARL TWEED

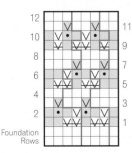

Foundation
Rows

L 3-st J
multiple

☐ With A, knit on right side, purl on wrong side

☐ With B, knit on right side, purl on wrong side

• With B, knit on wrong side

Ⅴ Slip 1 with yarn in back on right side, with yarn in front on wrong side

Ⅴ Slip 1 with yarn in front

Chapter 4

WALKING ON THE MOORS

Projects for Beginners

Accessories are almost always quicker to make than sweaters, and this chapter includes seven simple hats, scarves, and bags, all in tweed yarns. Easy pattern stitches and short repeats are the basis for these great designs, most of which can be knitted for either a man or a woman.

The projects in this chapter do call for some color combining, but it is done using the easiest of methods—working in stripes. Mind you, these are no ordinary stripes. The Lichen Ribbed Garter Scarf (page 42) has uneven color blocks, and the Kilt Knitting Bag (page 44) combines stripes in stockinette stitch with stripes in seed stitch.

The chapter ends with a beginner sweater that is perfect for new knitters or those looking for a beautiful but mindless knitting project.

North Sea Hat & Scarf Set

DESIGNED BY LINDA CYR

There are stripes, and then there are stripes. The uneven striping in Linda Cyr's hat-scarf duo creates a contemporary feel and works for either a man or a woman. Note that you can make the hat on straight needles and then seam the back, or you can use circular and double-pointed needles to eliminate the seam. This is a great first knitting project. Just practice the rib pattern before you begin—it's a simple two-row repeat. To make it even easier, mark the right side with a safety pin that you can move along as you knit.

BEGINNER seamed version
INTERMEDIATE circular version

KNITTED MEASUREMENTS

Scarf 5¾" wide x 62" long (14.5cm x 157.5cm)

Hat (both versions) 20" in circumference x 8½" tall (51cm x 21.5 cm)

MATERIALS

Note: Materials listed are sufficient to make both pieces.

3 balls Tahki Yarns Soho Tweed (100% pure new wool, 1¾ oz [50g], 55 yd [50m]) in #358 light gray (C) and 1 ball each in #336 black (A) and #304 charcoal (B) **(5)** bulky

Size 10 (6mm) needles, or size needed to obtain gauge

Size 10 (6mm) circular needle, 16" (40.5cm) long, or size needed to obtain gauge (for circular hat)

Size 10 (6mm) double-pointed needles (for circular hat)

Yarn needle

GAUGE

13 stitches and 19 rows = 4" (10cm) in rib pattern

TAKE TIME TO CHECK GAUGE.

SPECIAL TECHNIQUE

Edge Stitches With the yarn in front, slip the first stitch of every row purlwise, place the yarn to the back (knit position) *between* the needles, and work the next (knit) stitch.

Note: To keep slipped edge stitches neat when changing colors, work as follows: work across to the last stitch of the row, drop the old color, and then join the new color and knit the last stitch. Continue with the new color on the next row.

PATTERN STITCHES

Garter Stitch for Scarf and Seamed Version of Hat
Knit every row.

Garter Stitch for Circular Version of Hat
Knit 1 round, purl 1 round.

Rib Pattern for Scarf and Seamed Version of Hat
(multiple of 4 stitches + 2 extra stitches)
Row 1 (right side) Knit.
Row 2 K2, *p2, k2; repeat from * across.
Repeat rows 1 and 2 for rib pattern.

Rib Pattern for Circular Version of Hat
(multiple of 4 stitches)
Round 1 Knit.
Round 2 *K2, p2; repeat from * around.
Repeat rounds 1 and 2 for rib pattern.

SCARF

Using A, cast on 18 stitches.

(Right side) Begin garter stitch; work even for 4 rows, ending with a wrong-side row.

Begin Pattern

(Right side) Continuing with A, change to rib pattern and begin working edge stitches as follows:

Row 1 Slip 1 (edge stitch), knit to end.

Row 2 Slip 1 (edge stitch), k1 (these 2 stitches count as the first k2 of rib pattern); continuing from * of row 2 of rib pattern, work to end.

Continue to work rib pattern and edge stitches in this way (repeating rows 1 and 2) for the remainder of the scarf, and AT THE SAME TIME, work stripes as follows:

Work even until the piece measures 4" (10cm) from the beginning, ending with a wrong-side row and changing to B in the last stitch of the last row (see Special Technique on page 39).

Using B, work even in rib pattern until the B section measures 5" (12.5cm) from the color change, ending with a wrong-side row and changing to C in the last stitch.

Using C, work even in rib pattern until the C section measures 48" (122cm) from the color change, ending with a wrong-side row and changing to B in the last stitch.

Using B, work even in rib pattern until the B section measures 5" (12.5cm) from the color change, ending with a wrong-side row and changing to A in the last stitch.

Using A, work even in rib pattern until the A section measures 4" (10cm) from the color change, ending with a wrong-side row.

Knit 4 rows.

Bind off all stitches loosely.

FINISHING

Using the yarn needle, weave in all ends.

Steam-block, if necessary, being careful not to flatten the texture.

HAT
Seamed Version

Using A, cast on 66 stitches.

(Right side) Begin garter stitch; work even for 4 rows, ending with a wrong-side row.

(Right side) Begin rib pattern; continuing with A, work even for 8 rows, ending with a wrong-side row.

(Right side) Continuing in rib pattern, change to B; work even for 12 rows, ending with a wrong-side row.

(Right side) Continuing in rib pattern, change to C; work even for 6 rows, ending with a wrong-side row.

Shape Crown
Decrease Row (right side) *K2, k2tog; repeat from * across to the last 2 stitches, k2—50 stitches remain.

Row 2 K2, *p1, k2; repeat from * across.

Row 3 Knit.

Rows 4–8 Repeat rows 2 and 3 twice, then row 2 once more, ending with a wrong-side row.

Decrease Row (right side) *K2tog, k1; repeat from * across to the last 2 stitches, k2tog—33 stitches remain.

Rows 10, 12, 14, and 16 Purl.

Rows 11 and 13 Knit.

Row 15 K2tog across to the last stitch, k1—17 stitches remain.

Row 17 Repeat row 15—9 stitches remain.

Cut the yarn, leaving an 18" (45.5cm) tail. Using the yarn needle, thread the tail through the remaining stitches and pull tightly to close the top of the hat; fasten off securely on the wrong side, but *do not* cut the yarn. Using the remaining tail, sew the center back seam.

HAT
Circular Version

Using the circular needle and A, cast on 64 stitches. Join, being careful not to twist stitches; place a marker for the beginning of the round.

Begin garter stitch; work even for 4 rounds.

Change to rib pattern; continuing with A, work even for 8 rounds.

Continuing in rib pattern, change to B; work even for 12 rounds.

Continuing in rib pattern, change to C; work even for 6 rounds.

Shape Crown
Note: Change to double-pointed needles, as necessary, while working shaping.

Decrease Round *K2, k2tog; repeat from * around—48 stitches remain.

Round 2 *K2, p1; repeat from * around.

Round 3 Knit.

Rounds 4–8 Repeat rounds 2 and 3 twice, then round 2 once more.

Decrease Round *K1, ssk; repeat from * around—32 stitches remain.

Rounds 10–14 Knit.

Rounds 15 and 16 K2tog around—8 stitches remain.

Cut yarn, leaving a 12" (30.5cm) tail. Using the yarn needle, thread the tail through the remaining stitches and pull tightly to close the top of the hat. Fasten off securely on the wrong side.

FINISHING

Using the yarn needle, weave in the ends.

Steam-block, if necessary, being careful not to flatten the texture.

Lichen Ribbed Garter Scarf

DESIGNED BY NANCY J. THOMAS

The 100 percent wool here mimics traditional tweed in its woolen spun form, but without the nepps. Rather than nepps, the color comes from random striping. The garter stitch diamonds on each end are united with a flexible ribbed center to make the scarf more wearable.

If this is your first project or if you are as distracted a knitter as I am, keep track of rows. One easy way to know how many rows you've knit is to count the garter-stitch ridges as two rows equal one ridge.

EASY

KNITTED MEASUREMENTS
Length 40" (101.5cm)

MATERIALS

2 balls Filatura Di Crosa 127 Print (100% wool, 1¾ oz [50g], 93 yd [85m]) in #27 olive mix (**4**) medium

Size 10 (6mm) needles, or size needed to obtain gauge

Stitch markers

Yarn needle

GAUGE

20 stitches = 3½" (9cm) and 20 rows = 4" (10cm) in rib stitch

TAKE TIME TO CHECK GAUGE.

ABBREVIATIONS AND TERMS

k1-f/b Knit the next stitch, do not drop the stitch from the left-hand needle; knit the same stitch through the back loop, drop the stitch from the left-hand needle— 1 stitch increased.

PATTERN STITCHES

Note: Both garter stitch and k2, p2 rib look the same on either side; indications for the right side and the wrong side are for shaping purposes only.

Garter Stitch
Knit every row; 2 rows of garter stitch = 1 garter ridge.

K2, P2 Rib
(multiple of 4 stitches)
Row 1 (wrong side) *K2, p2; repeat from * across.
Row 2 Knit the knit stitches and purl the purl stitches as they face you. Repeat row 2 for k2, p2 rib.

Continue in garter stitch until there are a total of 25 garter ridges, ending with a wrong-side row.

Decrease Row (right side) Decrease 1 stitch by ssk, knit across to the last 2 stitches, decrease 1 stitch by k2tog—23 stitches remain.

(Wrong side) Knit 1 row even.

Repeat the last 2 rows 5 times, ending with a wrong-side row—13 stitches remain.

Center Section
Increase Row (right side) *K1-f/b, k1; repeat from * 5 times more, k1-f/b in last stitch—20 stitches; place a marker for the beginning of the center section.

(Wrong side) Change to k2, p2 rib; work even until the piece measures 21" (53.5cm) from the marker, ending with a right-side row.

Decrease Row (wrong side) *K2tog, k1; repeat from * across to last 2 stitches, k2tog—13 stitches remain; place a marker for the end of the center section.

Second End
Increase Row (right side) K1-f/b in first stitch, knit across to the last 2 stitches, k1-f/b in next stitch, k1—15 stitches.

(Wrong side) Knit 1 row even.

Repeat the last 2 rows 5 times—25 stitches.

Continue in garter stitch until there are 21 garter ridges from the end of the center section, ending with a wrong-side row.

Decrease Row (right side) Ssk, knit across to the last 2 stitches, k2tog—23 stitches remain.

(Wrong side) Knit 1 row even.

Repeat the last 2 rows 10 times—3 stitches remain.

Bind off the remaining stitches.

FINISHING

Using the yarn needle, weave in all ends.

SCARF

Cast on 3 stitches.

First End
(Wrong side) Begin garter stitch; knit 1 row even; place a marker at the beginning of the next row to indicate the beginning of a right-side row.

Increase Row (right side) Increase 1 stitch in first stitch by k1-f/b, knit across to the last 2 stitches, k1-f/b in next stitch, k1—5 stitches.

(Wrong side) Knit 1 row even.

Repeat the last 2 rows 10 times—25 stitches; 12 garter ridges.

Kilt Knitting Bag

DESIGNED BY NANCY J. THOMAS

With balls of leftover yarn from several projects, I decided to make a quick, beginner bag. The shades of green, grey, purple, and orange tweed reminded me of Ireland and Scotland.

Making this bag and felting it was the easy part; finding straps proved to be a challenge. Wanting something a little different, I headed for my hardware store. I looked at ropes and twine, but these were dull. Then I found lawn chair webbing. Bingo! After a short search, the young man brought out some dusty packages of brightly colored plastic fabric. I cut the lengths, folded them in half, and embroidered each strap with an easy running stitch.

BEGINNER

KNITTED MEASUREMENTS
12" x 18" (30.5cm x 45.5cm), after felting

MATERIALS
Note: You'll need only 1 skein (or less) of each color. Use leftover yarns from other tweed projects.

1 skein Tahki Yarns Donegal Tweed (100% wool, 3½ oz [100g], 183 yd [168m]) in #892 green (A), #893 orange (B), #884 light gray (C), #866 medium gray (D), #849 eggplant (E), and #867 taupe (F) medium

1 ball Tahki Yarns Shannon (100% wool, 1¾ oz [50g], 92 yd [85m]) in #14 red/orange mix (G)

Size 9 (5.5mm) and size 13 (9mm) needles, or size needed to obtain gauge

2 pieces 2¼" (5.5cm) wide lawn-chair webbing, each 30" (76cm) long

Yarn needle

GAUGE
11 stitches and 14 rows = 4" (10cm) in stockinette stitch, using the larger needles and 2 strands of yarn held together

TAKE TIME TO CHECK GAUGE.

PATTERN STITCHES
Stockinette Stitch
Knit on the right side, purl on the wrong side.

Garter Stitch
Knit every row; 2 rows of garter stitch = 1 garter ridge.

Seed Stitch
(multiple of 2 stitches)
Row 1 (right side) *K1, p1; repeat from * across.
Row 2 Purl the knit stitches and knit the purl stitches as they face you.
Repeat row 2 for seed stitch rib.

COLORWAYS
Green (A/A) = 2 strands of A.
Gray (C/D) = 1 strand each of C and D.
Eggplant (E/E) = 2 strands of E.
Taupe (F/F) = 2 strands of F.
Red/orange (B/G) = 1 strand each of B and G.

Note: The bag is worked using the larger needles and 2 strands of yarn held together throughout (see Colorways above); the Pocket is worked using the smaller needles and 1 strand of yarn.

ASSEMBLY

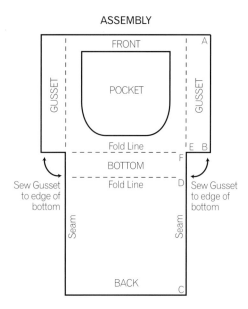

BACK

Using 2 strands of green (A/A), cast on 40 stitches.

(Wrong side) Knit 1 row.

(Right side) Begin garter stitch; knit 4 rows (2 garter ridges), ending with a wrong-side row.

(Right side) Change to stockinette stitch; continuing with A/A, work even for 4 rows.

(Right side) Change to seed stitch and red/orange (B/G); work even for 2 rows.

(Right side) Change to stockinette stitch and gray (C/D); work even for 8 rows.

(Right side) Change to seed stitch and B/G; work even for 2 rows.

(Right side) Change to stockinette stitch and eggplant (E/E); work even for 8 rows.

(Right side) Change to seed stitch and B/G; work even for 2 rows.

(Right side) Change to stockinette stitch and A/A; work even for 8 rows.

(Right side) Change to seed stitch and B/G; work even for 2 rows.

(Right side) Change to stockinette stitch and C/D; work even for 8 rows.

(Right side) Change to seed stitch and B/G; work even for 2 rows.

BOTTOM

(Right side) Change to garter stitch and taupe (F/F); work even for 16 rows (8 garter ridges), ending with a wrong-side row.

FRONT

(Right side) Using B/G, cast on 10 stitches at the beginning of this row; change to seed stitch and work across 40 stitches on the needle—50 stitches.

(Wrong side) Continuing with B/G, cast on 10 stitches at the beginning of the row; work across 50 stitches on the needle in seed stitch—60 stitches.

(Right side) Change to stockinette stitch and C/D; work even for 8 rows.

(Right side) Change to seed stitch and B/G; work even for 2 rows.

(Right side) Change to stockinette stitch and A/A; work even for 8 rows.

(Right side) Change to seed stitch and B/G; work even for 2 rows.

(Right side) Change to stockinette stitch and eggplant (E/E); work even for 8 rows.

(Right side) Change to seed stitch and B/G; work even for 2 rows.

(Right side) Change to stockinette stitch and C/D; work even for 8 rows.

(Right side) Change to seed stitch and B/G; work even for 2 rows.

(Right side) Change to stockinette stitch and A/A; work even for 4 rows.

(Right side) Change to garter stitch; continuing with A/A, knit 4 rows (2 garter ridges).

Bind off all stitches.

POCKET

Beginning at the lower edge of the Pocket, using the smaller needles and 1 strand of A, cast on 25 stitches.

(Wrong side) Begin garter stitch; knit 3 rows, ending with a wrong-side row.

(Right side) Change to stockinette stitch; beginning

this row, increase 1 stitch each side every other row 7 times—39 stitches.

Work even until the piece measures 8" (20.5cm) from the beginning, ending with a wrong-side row.

Upper Edge of Pocket
(Right side) Change to garter stitch and 1 strand of D; knit 8 rows (4 garter ridges).

Bind off all stitches.

ASSEMBLY (SEE THE DIAGRAM)

Sew the side seams (sew A/B of the side gusset to C/D of the first side on both sides of the Bag, matching the pattern); sew the 10 cast-on stitches (the lower edge of the side gusset—E/B) to the edges of the Bag bottom (D/F).

FINISHING

Felt Bag and Pocket
See the felting instructions on page 23.

Attach Pocket
After the pieces have dried, center the Pocket onto the second side of the Bag and pin in place; using the yarn needle and matching yarn, stitch in place along the sides and lower edge of the Pocket.

Straps
Fold each 30" (76cm) piece of webbing in half lengthwise. Using the yarn needle and A, stitch the doubled webbing together using a running stitch. Beginning 2" (5cm) down from the upper edge of the inside of the Bag, sew the straps securely in place.

Highlands Felted Bag & Beret

DESIGNED BY LINDA CYR

This paisley bag is the perfect accompaniment to the dotted beret. The knitting and felting is simple. Add the appliqués, attach the metal rings, and add the belt handle—then you're ready to go!

INTERMEDIATE

KNITTED MEASUREMENTS

Bag 14½" (37cm) wide x 11" (28cm) tall x 4" (10cm) deep

Beret Approximately 9" in diameter x 3½" deep (23cm x 9cm)

MATERIALS

8 balls Tahki Yarns Soho Tweed (100% pure new wool, 1¾ oz [50g], 55 yd [50m]) in #304 charcoal (MC) (5) bulky

1 skein Tahki Yarns Donegal Tweed (100% pure new wool, 3½ oz [100g], 183 yd [167m]) each in #874 burgundy (A), #843 blue (B), #896 purple (C), #892 green (D), and #893 pumpkin (E) (4) medium

Note: Yarn amounts are enough for both pieces.

Size 10 (6mm) circular needle, 24" (61cm) long, or size needed to obtain gauge

Size J-10 (6mm) crochet hook

Stitch markers

Yarn needle

1 wooden toggle button, 1" (25mm)

½ yard (0.5m) fabric for lining (optional)

6" (15cm) grosgrain ribbon, ¾" (2cm) wide, for handle loops

2 metal rings, 1½" (4cm) in diameter

Sewing needle and thread

Store-bought thin leather belt, 45" (114cm) long (for handle)

GAUGE

12 stitches and 19 rounds = 4" (10cm) in stockinette stitch

TAKE TIME TO CHECK GAUGE.

SPECIAL TECHNIQUES

Short-Row Shaping Work the number of stitches indicated in the instructions, turn; return to starting point. Continue to work progressively shorter rows as indicated in the instructions; each short row is worked as 2 rows—one on the right side, one on the wrong side.

Edge Stitches With the yarn in front, slip the first stitch purlwise, yarn back, work across to the last stitch, and knit the last stitch.

Note: The last stitch of every row will be knit as part of the stitch pattern.

PATTERN STITCHES

Chain

Begin by making a slip knot on the crochet hook. Wrap the yarn around the hook (yarn over), and draw it through the loop on the hook to form the first chain. Repeat this step as many times as instructed. (The loop on the hook is never included when counting the number of chains.)

Double Crochet

Yarn over the hook, insert the hook into the indicated stitch, yarn over and pull up a loop, [yarn over and draw through two loops on the hook] twice.

Garter Stitch

Knit every row.

Half Double Crochet

Yarn over the hook, insert the hook into the indicated stitch, yarn over and pull up a loop, yarn over and draw through all three loops on the hook.

Single Crochet

Insert the hook in the indicated stitch, yarn over and pull up a loop, yarn over and draw through both loops on the hook.

Slip Stitch

Insert the hook in the indicated stitch, yarn over and draw through both the stitch and the loop on the hook.

Stockinette Stitch

Knit on the right side, purl on the wrong side.

Treble Crochet

Yarn over the hook 2 times, insert the hook in the indicated stitch, yarn over and pull up a loop, [yarn over and draw through 2 loops] 3 times.

Note: While working the bottom of the Bag, slip the first stitch purlwise (edge stitch) on every row; this will make it easier to pick up the stitches along the row ends for working the main section of the Bag in the round.

BAG

BOTTOM OF BAG

Using MC, cast on 51 stitches.

(Right side) Begin garter stitch, slipping the first stitch of every row (see the note above). Work even for 32 rows.

BAG SIDES

Joining Round Slip 1, knit across 50 stitches, pick up and knit 16 stitches along the row ends (in slipped edge stitches), 50 stitches along the cast-on edge, and 15 stitches along the row ends of the remaining side, knit the slip stitch at the beginning of round; place a marker for the beginning of round—132 stitches; 50 stitches each for Front and Back, 16 stitches for each side of the gusset.

Rounds 2–9 Begin garter stitch (purl 1 round, knit 1 round); work even for 8 rounds; *do not* work the last stitch of round 9.

Shape Gussets

Round 10 Working the last stitch of the previous round together with the first stitch of this round, *k2tog, place a marker, k48, ssk, k14 (side gusset); repeat from * once—128 stitches remain.

Rounds 11–16 Work even in stockinette stitch (knit every round).

Round 17 K2tog, k48, ssk, knit to 2 before marker, k2tog, slip marker, k48, ssk, knit to end of round—124 stitches remain.

Rounds 18–23 Work even in stockinette stitch.

Rounds 24–58 Repeat rounds 17–23—104 stitches remain.

Round 59 Repeat round 17—100 stitches remain.

Bind off all stitches.

PAISLEYS

Make 2 each in the following color combinations: ADB, BEA, CAD, DCE, and EBC.

Using the hook and the first color, chain 2.

Round 1 Chain 1, work 6 single crochet in second chain from hook, join with a slip stitch to first stitch.

Round 2 Chain 1, work 2 single crochet in each stitch around, join with a slip stitch in first stitch—12 single crochet.

Round 3 Join the second color with a slip stitch in the same stitch as joining; chain 1, work [half double crochet, 2 double crochet, treble crochet] in same stitch, 3 single crochet along left side of treble crochet just completed, work [2 single crochet in next stitch, single crochet in next stitch] 5 times, work [4 single crochet, double crochet, half double crochet] in next stitch, join with a slip stitch in first stitch.

Round 4 Join the third color with a slip stitch in the same stitch as joining, chain 2, work [3 double crochet, half double crochet] in next stitch, work [single crochet next stitch, half double crochet next stitch, 3 double crochet in next stitch, half double crochet in next stitch] 6 times, single crochet in each of next 2 stitches, join with a slip stitch to second ch of starting chain-2.

Fasten off.

LOOP AND STEMS

Make 1 using MC (for the button loop) and 2 each using A, B, C, D, and E (for the stems).

Using the crochet hook and 2 strands of the appropriate color, work a chain 12" (30.5cm) long.

Fasten off.

FINISHING

Using the yarn needle, weave in all ends.

Felt all pieces, following the instructions on page 23.

Arrange the Paisley motifs as shown in the photo; sew in place.

Curl the stems and sew in place (see photo).

Button Loop

Knot the ends of the loop together, and sew at the center upper edge on the back; sew the button in place opposite the loop on the front.

Lining (optional)

Using the Bag as a pattern, cut the Lining fabric to fit, allowing ½" (13mm) for the side seams and at upper edge. Sew the Lining seams. With the right sides facing each other, insert the Lining into the Bag; fold under the seam allowance at the upper edge. Pin the Lining to the Bag.

Handle Loops

Cut the 6" (15cm) ribbon in half; fold each piece in half. Place the rings on the ribbons, and sew them in place on the wrong side at each side on the upper edge of the Lining. Using the sewing needle and thread, stitch the Lining neatly along the upper edge of the Bag. Thread the belt through the loops, and secure.

BERET

Note: The Crown is worked in wedges, using the short-row shaping technique; the remainder of the beret is worked in the round.

Using MC, cast on 14 stitches for crown.

FIRST WEDGE

Note: Work the first stitch of every row as given for edge stitches (see Special Techniques on page 48).

Row 1 Slip 1 (edge stitch), knit across.

Row 2 and all even-numbered rows Slip 1 (edge stitch), knit across.

Row 3 Slip 1, k11, turn.

Row 5 Slip 1, k9, turn.

Rows 7, 9, 11, and 13 Continue in this way, working 2 fewer stitches on each odd-numbered row—2 stitches worked on row 13.

Repeat row 2—wedge completed.

Work as for row 1, working across all stitches.

Work 12 more wedges as for the first wedge, ending by working the last row as for row 1 across all stitches.

Bind off all stitches.

Sew the bound-off edge to the cast-on edge to form a circle.

LOWER EDGE

Begin working in the round.

Round 1 With right side facing, pick up and p91 around outer edge of the crown; place a marker for the beginning of the round.

Rounds 2–7 Knit.

Round 8 *K11, k2tog; repeat from * around—84 stitches remain.

Rounds 9–12 Knit.

Round 13 *K10, k2tog; repeat from * around—77 stitches remain.

Rounds 14–15 Knit.

Rounds 16–18 Purl.

Bind off all stitches.

DOTS

Make 3 each in the following color combinations: AD, BE, CA, DC, and EB.

Using the hook and the appropriate color, chain 2.

Round 1 Chain 1, work 6 single crochet in second chain from hook, join with a slip stitch to first stitch.

Round 2 Chain 1, work 2 single crochet in each stitch around, join with a slip stitch in first stitch—12 single crochet.

Round 3 Join second color; chain 1, *work 2 single crochet in first stitch, single crochet in next stitch; repeat from * around, join with a slip stitch in first stitch.

Fasten off.

FINISHING

Using the yarn needle, weave in all ends.

Felt the hat, following the instructions on page 23.

Arrange the Dots as shown in the photo or as desired; sew in place.

Gaelic Hat

DESIGNED BY LINDA CYR

Make a fashion statement with this jaunty, oversized stocking hat. The bulky tweed yarn offers more visual tweed flecks than those in a finer-weight yarn. For beginners, try making the hat with straight needles and a back seam. If you are comfortable with circular and double-pointed needles, make it in the round.

BEGINNER seamed version
INTERMEDIATE circular version

KNITTED MEASUREMENTS

22" circumference x 14" tall (56cm x 35.5cm)

MATERIALS

1 ball Tahki Yarns Soho Tweed (100% pure new wool, 1¾ oz [50g], 55 yd [50m]) each in #336 black (A), #309 red (B), and #354 olive (C) ⑤ bulky

Size 10 (6mm) needles, or size needed to obtain gauge (for seamed version)

Size 10 (6mm) circular needle, 24" (60cm) long, or size needed to obtain gauge (for circular version)

Size 10 (6mm) double-pointed needles (for circular version)

Yarn needle

Stitch marker

Pom-pom maker or piece of cardboard

GAUGE

12 stitches and 22 rows = 4" (10cm) in garter stitch rib

TAKE TIME TO CHECK GAUGE.

PATTERN STITCHES (see charts)

K1, P1 Rib for Seamed Version (multiple of 2 stitches)
Row 1 K1 (seam stitch), *k1, p1; repeat from * across to the last stitch, k1 (seam stitch).
Repeat row 1 for k1, p1 rib, working the seam stitches in garter stitch (knit every row).

K1, P1 Rib for Circular Version (multiple of 2 stitches)
Round 1 *K1, p1; repeat from * around.
Repeat round 1 for k1, p1 rib.

K1, P1 RIB

2-st repeat

Garter Stitch Rib for Seamed Version (multiple of 4 stitches + 2 extra stitches)
Row 1 and all right-side rows Knit.
Rows 2 and 4 K1 (seam stitch), *p1, k3; repeat from * across to the last stitch, k1 (seam stitch).
Rows 6 and 8 K1 (seam stitch), *k2, p1, k1; repeat from * across to the last stitch, k1 (seam stitch).
Repeat rows 1–8 for garter rib, working the seam stitches in garter stitch (knit every row).

Garter Stitch Rib for Circular Version (multiple of 4 stitches)
Round 1 and all odd-numbered rounds Knit.
Rounds 2 and 4 *P3, k1; repeat from * around.
Rounds 6 and 8 P1, *k1, p3; repeat from * around to last 3 stitches, k1, p2.
Repeat rounds 1–8 for garter rib.

GARTER RIB

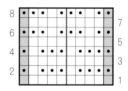

4-st rep

Note: **Circular Version** Work all rounds from right to left.
Seamed Version Work right-side rows from right to left, work wrong-side rows from left to right.

☐ Knit on right side, purl on wrong side
⊡ Purl on right side, knit on wrong side
▢ Seam stitch (for Seamed Version only)

Seamed Version

Note: The charts include the seam stitches; work the seam stitch and then work the repeat as indicated, ending the row with a seam stitch.

Using A, cast on 66 stitches.

(Right side) Begin k1, p1 rib; work even until the piece measures 5" (12.5cm) from the beginning, ending with a wrong-side row; fasten off A.

(Right side) Change to garter rib; using B, work even for 16 rows; using C, work even for 16 rows; using A, work even for 8 rows, ending with a wrong-side row.

Shape Crown

Note: Continue working 1 stitch each side in garter stitch (seam stitches) while shaping the crown.

Row 1 (right side) K1, *k2tog, k2; repeat from * across to the last stitch, k1—50 stitches remain.

Row 2 K1, *p1, k2; repeat from * across to the last stitch, k1.

Row 3 K1, *k1, k2tog; repeat from * across to the last stitch, k1—34 stitches remain.

Rows 4 and 6 K1, *p1, k1; repeat from * across to the last stitch, k1.

Row 5 K1, *k2tog; repeat from * across to the last stitch, k1—18 stitches remain.

Row 7 Repeat row 5—10 stitches remain.

Cut the yarn, leaving an 18" (45.5cm) yarn end. Using the yarn needle, thread the yarn end through the remaining stitches on the needle; pull tightly to close the hole, and fasten securely. Use the remaining yarn end to sew the back seam.

Circular Version

Note: The charts include seam stitches for the Seamed Version; do not work those stitches for the Circular Version.

Using A, cast on 64 stitches. Join, being careful not to twist stitches; place a marker for the beginning of the round.

Begin k1, p1 rib; work even until the piece measures 5" (12.5cm) from the beginning; fasten off A.

Change to garter rib; using B, work even for 16 rounds; using C, work even for 16 rounds; using A, work even for 8 rounds.

Shape Crown

Change to double-pointed needles as needed.

Round 1 *K2tog, k2; repeat from * around—48 stitches remain.

Round 2 *P2, k1; repeat from * around.

Round 3 *K1, k2tog; repeat from * around—32 stitches remain.

Rounds 4 and 6 *P1, k1; repeat from * around.

Round 5 *K2tog; repeat from * around—16 stitches remain.

Round 7 Repeat round 5—8 stitches remain.

Cut the yarn, leaving a 12" (30.5cm) yarn end. Using the yarn needle, thread the yarn end through the remaining stitches on the needle; pull tightly to close the hole, and fasten off securely.

FINISHING

Steam-block the hat, if necessary, being careful not to flatten the texture.

Using the yarn needle, weave in all ends.

POM-POM

Using a pom-pom maker or a piece of cardboard, make a pom-pom 5" (12.5cm) in diameter.

Note: The pom-pom shown in the photo was made with 80 wraps of B and 5 wraps each of A and C.

Attach the pom-pom to the top of the hat.

Tweed River Pullover

DESIGNED BY POONAM THAKUR

This beautiful sweater is made not in traditional tweed but, rather, in a wool yarn with a lightly spun roving wrapped with two thin, solid strands and one thin, multi-color strand. The quality of the 100 percent wool will make this pullover a long-lasting favorite that you'll wear for years to come. It's a great sweater style for either a girl or a guy, and it comes in multiple sizes.

BEGINNER

SIZES

Small (Medium, Large, 1X, 2X)

KNITTED MEASUREMENTS

Bust 34½ (38, 42½, 46, 50½)" (87.5 [96.5, 108, 117, 128.5]cm)

Length 21 (22, 23, 24, 24½)" (51 [53.5, 56, 58.5, 59.5]cm)

MATERIALS

9 (10, 11, 12, 13) balls Tahki Yarns Shannon (100% wool, 1¾ oz [50g], 92 yd [84m]) in #21 lavender multi (4) medium

Size 7 (4.5mm) and size 9 (5.5mm) needles, or size needed to obtain gauge

Size 7 (4.5mm) circular needle, 16" (40.5cm) long (for Circular Version of neck band) (optional)

Stitch markers

Stitch holders

Yarn needle

GAUGE

18 stitches and 24 rows = 4" (10cm) in stockinette stitch, using the larger needles

TAKE TIME TO CHECK GAUGE.

PATTERN STITCHES

K2, P2 Rib

(multiple of 4 stitches + 2 extra stitches)

Row 1 (right side) K2, *p2, k2; repeat from * across.

Row 2 Knit the knit stitches and purl the purl stitches as they face you.

Repeat row 2 for k2, p2 rib.

Stockinette Stitch

Knit on the right side, purl on the wrong side.

3 (3¼, 3½, 4, 4¾)"
7 (7½, 8, 8, 8½)"
1"
3½"
7½ (8, 8½, 9, 9½)"
21 (22, 23, 24, 24½)"
BACK AND FRONT
12½ (13, 13½, 14, 14)"
17¼ (19, 21, 22¾, 25¼)"

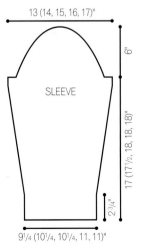

13 (14, 15, 16, 17)"
6"
SLEEVE
17 (17½, 18, 18, 18)"
2¾"
9¼ (10¼, 10¼, 11, 11)"

Note: For ease in working, circle the numbers that pertain to your size.

BACK

Using the larger needles, cast on 78 (86, 94, 102, 114) stitches.

(Right side) Begin k2, p2 rib; work even until the piece measures 1½" (4cm) from the beginning, ending with a wrong-side row.

(Right side) Change to stockinette stitch; work even until the piece measures 12½ (13, 13½, 14, 14)" (32 [33, 34.5, 35.5, 35.5]cm) from the beginning, ending with a wrong-side row.

Shape Armhole

(Right side) Bind off 4 (4, 4, 5, 5) stitches at the beginning of the next 2 rows, then 2 (3, 4, 4, 6) stitches at the beginning of the next 2 rows—66 (72, 78, 84, 92) stitches remain.

(Right side) Decrease 1 stitch each side every other row 3 (4, 5, 6, 7) times—60 (64, 68, 72, 78) stitches remain.

Work even until the armhole measures 7½ (8, 8½, 9, 9½)" (19 [20.5, 21.5, 23, 24]cm) from the beginning of the shaping, ending with a wrong-side row; place a marker at each side of the center 22 (24, 26, 26, 28) stitches.

Shape Neck and Shoulder

Right Shoulder With the right side facing, work across to the first marker; place the center stitches on a holder for the neck; place the remaining 19 (20, 21, 23, 25) stitches on a separate holder for the left shoulder, turn.

(Wrong side) At the neck edge, bind off 3 stitches, work to end, turn—16 (17, 18, 20, 22) stitches remain.

(Right side) At the shoulder edge, bind off 7 (8, 8, 9, 10) stitches, work to end, turn—9 (9, 10, 11, 12) stitches remain.

(Wrong side) At the neck edge, bind off 2 stitches, work to end, turn—7 (7, 8, 9, 10) stitches remain.

(Right side) At the shoulder edge, bind off the remaining stitches.

Left Shoulder With the right side facing, place 19 (20, 21, 23, 25) stitches from the left shoulder holder on a needle, ready to work a right-side row; knit to end, turn.

(Wrong side) Work 1 row even, turn.

Work the shaping as for the right neck and shoulder, reversing the shaping by working the neck shaping at the beginning of the right-side rows and the shoulder shaping at the beginning of the wrong-side rows.

FRONT

Using the larger needles, cast on 78 (86, 94, 102, 114) stitches.

Work as for the Back until the armhole measures 5 (5½, 6, 6½, 7)" (12.5 [14, 15, 16.5, 18]cm) from the beginning of the shaping, ending with a wrong-side row—60 (64, 68, 72, 78) stitches remain; place a marker at each side of the center 12 (14, 16, 16, 18) stitches.

Shape Neck

Left Neck Shaping With the right side facing, work across to the marker; place the center stitches on a holder for the neck; place the remaining 24 (25, 26, 28, 30) stitches on a separate holder for the right neck and shoulder, turn.

(Wrong side) At the neck edge, bind off 3 stitches, work to end, turn—21 (22, 23, 25, 27) stitches remain.

(Right side) Work 1 row even.

(Wrong side) At the neck edge, bind off 2 stitches, work to end, turn—19 (20, 21, 23, 25) stitches remain.

(Right side) Work 1 row even.

(Wrong side) At the neck edge, decrease 1 stitch every other row 5 times, working the armhole edge (right-side rows) even—14 (15, 16, 18, 20) stitches remain. Work even until the armhole measures the same as the Back to the beginning of the shoulder shaping, ending with a wrong-side row.

Shape Shoulder

(Right side) At the shoulder edge, bind off 7 (8, 8, 9, 10) stitches, work to end, turn—7 (7, 8, 9, 10) stitches remain.

(Wrong side) Work 1 row even.

(Right side) Bind off the remaining stitches.

Right Neck Shaping With the right side facing, place 24 (25, 26, 28, 30) stitches from the right neck and shoulder holder on a needle, ready to work a right-side row; knit to end, turn.

(Wrong side) Work 1 row even, turn.

Work the shaping as for the left neck, reversing the shaping by working decreases at the beginning of the right-side rows. Work even until the armhole measures the same as the Back to the beginning of the shoulder shaping, ending with a right-side row.

Shape Shoulder

(Wrong side) At the shoulder edge, bind off 7 (8, 8, 9, 10) stitches, work to end, turn—7 (7, 8, 9, 10) stitches remain.

(Right side) Work 1 row even.

(Wrong side) Bind off the remaining stitches.

SLEEVES (MAKE 2)

Using the smaller needles, cast on 42 (46, 46, 50, 50) stitches.

(Right side) Begin k2, p2 rib, ending k2; work even until the piece measures 2¾" (7cm) from the beginning, ending with a wrong-side row.

(Right side) Changing to the larger needles and stockinette stitch, work even for 8 (8, 6, 6, 8) rows, ending with a wrong-side row.

Shape Sleeve

(Right side) Continue in stockinette stitch; beginning this row, increase 1 stitch each side every 8 (8, 8, 8, 6) rows 9 (9, 11, 11, 13) times, working the increased stitches in stockinette stitch—60 (64, 68, 72, 76) stitches.

Work even until the piece measures 17 (17½, 18, 18, 18)" (43 [44.5, 45.5, 45.5, 45.5]cm) from the beginning, ending with a wrong-side row.

Shape Cap

(Right side) Bind off 4 (4, 4, 5, 5) stitches at the beginning of the next 2 rows, then 2 (3, 4, 4, 6) stitches at the beginning of the next 2 rows—48 (50, 52, 54, 54) stitches remain.

(Right side) Decrease 1 stitch each side every other row 15 times—18 (20, 22, 24, 24) stitches remain.

(Right side) Bind off 3 (4, 5, 6, 6) stitches at the beginning of the next 2 rows—12 stitches remain.

Bind off the remaining stitches.

FINISHING

Block the pieces to the measurements.

Neck Band (Seamed Version)

Sew the right shoulder seam.

With the right side facing, using the smaller needles, join the yarn at the left Front shoulder; pick up and knit 17 stitches down the left neck shaping; knit 12 (14, 16, 16, 18) stitches from the Front holder; pick up and knit 16 stitches up the right Front neck shaping to the shoulder; pick up and knit 5 stitches along the Back neck to the holder; knit 22 (24, 26, 26, 28) stitches from the holder; pick up and knit 6 stitches to the left shoulder—78 (82, 86, 86, 90) stitches.

(Wrong side) Beginning and ending p2, work even in k2, p2 rib until the neck band measures 3½" (9cm) from the pickup row, ending with a wrong-side row.

Bind off all stitches loosely in rib.

Sew the left shoulder and neck band seam.

Neck Band (Circular Version)

Sew the shoulder seams.

With the right side facing, using the circular needle, pick up and knit 76 (80, 84, 84, 88) stitches evenly around the neck shaping, including the stitches on holders; place a marker for the beginning of the round. (Refer to the instructions above for the Seamed Version as a guide to picking up the stitches.)

Begin k2, p2 rib; work even until the neck band measures 3½" (9cm) from the pickup round.

Bind off the remaining stitches loosely in rib.

Set in the Sleeves, matching the shaping; sew the side and sleeve seams.

Using the yarn needle, weave in all ends.

Chapter 5

HIKING THE SCOTTISH UPLANDS

Projects for Advanced Beginners

Now that you've created the easier accessories, it's time to move on to five exciting projects that will stretch your skills and allow you to experiment further with tweed yarns. Included in this chapter are a home décor piece, a cabled scarf, one pullover in a heavyweight tweed wool, a lightweight bicolor vest, and a two-toned cardigan with fun tie fronts. Other than relatively easy cabling and ribbing, all the projects are fairly simple.

Here you'll see firsthand that tweed yarns go hand in hand with cables. As you begin to make sweaters in this chapter, you'll have more details to consider. Start out by carefully checking your gauge to ensure the correct sweater size. Then look at the schematics of the sweater pieces to choose the size that you want to make. One easy way to figure out the desired size is to compare the given measurements on the schematic with your favorite sweater. Keep in mind that lighter-weight yarns drape and look different from sweaters made with thicker yarns. Although thicker yarns are great for quick knitting, they make better outerwear sweaters than those for inside wearing.

Coastal Cabled Scarf

DESIGNED BY LINDA CYR

Traditional tweed yarn has the "body" that makes cables stand out. For this scarf, Linda uses a braided cable made by twisting stitches on two different rows over the fourteen-stitch panel. Because there is no shaping, a scarf is a good way to try out a stitch pattern. For ease, keep the cable pattern marked off with stitch markers. As you work, keep track of the rows with a row counter or simple check marks on paper to make sure you twist the cables on the correct rows.

EASY

KNITTED MEASUREMENTS

Width 5¾" (14.5cm)

Length 70" (178cm)

MATERIALS

5 balls Tahki Yarns Soho Tweed (100% pure new wool, 1¾ oz [50g], 55yd [50m]) in #301 light gray (**6**) bulky

Size 10 (6mm) needles, or size needed to obtain gauge

Stitch markers

Cable needle

Yarn needle

GAUGE

13 stitches and 19 rows = 4" (10cm) in seed stitch; 14-stitch cable panel measures 2½" (6.5cm) wide

TAKE TIME TO CHECK GAUGE.

SPECIAL TECHNIQUE

Edge Stitches Slip the first stitch of every row knitwise, purl the last stitch.

Note: The last stitch of every row will be purled as part of the seed stitch border.

ABBREVIATIONS AND TERMS

C8B Slip 4 stitches onto a cable needle, hold to the back, knit 4 stitches, knit 4 stitches from the cable needle.

C8F Slip 4 stitches onto a cable needle, hold to the front, knit 4 stitches, knit 4 stitches from the cable needle.

PATTERN STITCHES

Seed Stitch Border

(panel of 4 stitches)

Row 1 (right side) *K1, p1; repeat from * once.

Row 2 Knit the purl stitches and purl the knit stitches as they face you. Repeat row 2 for seed stitch.

Cable

(panel of 14 stitches)

Row 1 (right side) P1, k12, p1.

Row 2 and all wrong-side rows K1, p12, k1.

Row 3 P1, C8B, k4, p1.

Row 7 P1, k4, C8F, p1.

Row 8 Repeat row 2.

Repeat rows 1–8 for cable.

CABLE CHART

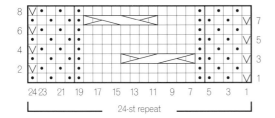

8																							7
6																							5
4																							3
2																							1

24 23   21   19   17   15   13   11   9   7   5   3   1

24-st repeat

☐   Knit on right side, purl on wrong side

⊡   Purl on right side, knit on wrong side

☑   Slip 1

⤬   C8B

⤬   C8F

SCARF

Cast on 24 stitches.

(Right side) Slip 1 (edge stitch), beginning row 1 of cable chart, work seed stitch across the next 4 stitches, place a marker; work cable across center 14 stitches; place a marker, p1, work in seed stitch to end.

Continue in this way until the piece measures 70" (178cm) from the beginning, ending with a wrong-side row.

Bind off all stitches loosely in pattern.

FINISHING

If necessary, block the piece lightly, being careful not to flatten the texture.

Using the yarn needle, weave in all ends.

Kilcar Felted Pillow

DESIGNED BY LINDA CYR

Although this pillow has an intermediate skill level, it's easy if you consider it as three sections—Front, Back, and edging.

The diamond-like Kilim pattern resembles the designs of many cultures—for example, it could be a Native American or a Middle Eastern design. In slightly different colors, the pattern might be Scandinavian or even Scottish.

The color pattern on the Front of the pillow is worked using the intarsia method, in which the yarns are not carried across the back of the work (as in the Fair Isle method). Since the color changes are simple, this is easy intarsia knitting. Any unevenness caused by changing colors is eliminated once the pillow is felted. The striped Back gives you a break from the intarsia Front.

INTERMEDIATE

KNITTED MEASUREMENTS

17½" (44.5cm) square (including the edging), after felting

MATERIALS

1 skein Tahki Yarns Donegal Tweed (100% pure new wool, 3½ oz [100g], 183 yd [167m]) each in #866 medium gray (A), #869 brown (B), #890 black (C), #863 red (D), and #867 taupe (E) (4) medium

Size 10 (6mm) needles, or size needed to obtain gauge

Size J-10 (6mm) crochet hook

Yarn needle

Bobbins (optional)

14" (35.5cm) square pillow form

GAUGE

14 stitches and 20 rows = 4" (10cm) in stockinette stitch, before felting

TAKE TIME TO CHECK GAUGE.

SPECIAL TECHNIQUE

Intarsia Method Work from the chart in stockinette stitch, using a separate ball or bobbin of yarn for each section; do not strand the colors not in use across the wrong side of the piece. As you begin each new section, twist the new color around the color just completed to prevent holes.

PATTERN STITCHES

Stockinette Stitch
Knit on the right side, purl on the wrong side.

Chain
Wrap the yarn around the crochet hook (yarn over) and draw it through the loop on the hook to form the first chain.

Single Crochet
Insert the crochet hook in the stitch, yarn over and pull up a loop, yarn over and draw through both loops on the hook.

Stripe Sequence
*In stockinette stitch, work 8 rows A, 8 rows B; repeat from * for stripe sequence.

Notes: The Front of the pillow is worked in the intarsia method; the Back is worked following the stripe sequence.

Wind bobbins for the small color areas to help keep the yarn from becoming tangled.

FRONT

Using A, cast on 52 stitches.

(Right side) Begin stockinette stitch; work even for 8 rows (rows 1–8 of the chart), ending with a wrong-side row.

Fasten off A.

Begin Pattern from Chart

Row 9 Join B, k17; join C, k18; join a second ball of B, k17.

Working in the intarsia method, changing colors as indicated, work rows 10–64 of the chart.

Fasten off all remaining colors.

Change to A; continuing in stockinette stitch, work even for 8 rows (rows 65–72 of the chart).

Bind off all stitches.

BACK

Using A, cast on 52 stitches.

(Right side) Begin the stripe sequence; work even for 72 rows, ending with 8 rows using A.

Bind off all stitches.

FINISHING

Place the Front and Back together, with the wrong sides together.

Join Front to Back

With the right side of the Front facing, using the crochet hook and C, begin at the upper-right-hand corner of the bound-off edge; working through both thicknesses, join the yarn with a slip stitch in the corner stitch of both pieces.

Round 1 Chain 1, beginning in the same stitch as joining, work 51 single crochet across the bound-off edges; work 3 single crochet in the corner stitch; join the row ends along the side edge by working 50 single crochet evenly down the side edge to the corner, [work 2 rows together approximately every third and fourth row]; work 3 single crochet in the corner stitch; work 30 single crochet across the cast-on edge through both thicknesses, then work single crochet in next 20 stitches on the Front only (to create the opening for the pillow form); work 3 single crochet for the corner stitch; join the remaining side as for the first side; work 2 single crochet in the same stitch as joining for the fourth corner, join with a slip stitch to the first single crochet.

Edging

Round 2 Chain 1, single crochet in each single crochet around, working 3 single crochet in center stitch at each corner.

Repeat round 2 until the edging measures 2" (5cm) from round 1.

Fasten off.

Use the yarn needle to weave in any ends that come loose during the felting process or to tighten any loose places between colors; it is not necessary to weave in all ends, as they will be secured during the felting process.

Felt the piece following the instructions on page 23.

Insert the pillow form; using the yarn needle threaded with C, neatly sew the opening closed.

FRONT CHART

☐ **Yarn A** Knit on right side, purl on wrong side

◆ **Yarn B** Knit on right side, purl on wrong side

▨ **Yarn C** Knit on right side, purl on wrong side

▨ **Yarn D** Knit on right side, purl on wrong side

☐ **Yarn E** Knit on right side, purl on wrong side

Carrick Pullover

DESIGNED BY POONAM THAKUR

How many times have you looked for a sweater that's warm enough for outdoor wear in cool weather yet isn't too fussy or formal looking? The clean lines of the rib-pattern turtleneck are flattering and simple. It's an easy knit, and the bulky-weight tweed makes it a quick project to complete. With the look and feel of an ageless tweed fabric, this earthy olive shade is a classic.

EASY

SIZES

X-Small (Small, Medium, Large, 1X, 2X)

KNITTED MEASUREMENTS

Bust 35 (38, 41½, 45, 48½, 52)" (89 [96.5, 105.5, 114, 123, 132]cm)

Length 21 (22, 23, 23½, 24, 24½)" (53.5 [56, 58.5, 59.5, 61, 62]cm)

MATERIALS

13 (14, 15, 16, 17, 18) balls Tahki Yarns Soho Tweed (100% pure new wool, 1¾ oz [50g], 55 yd [50m]) in #357 olive (5) bulky

Size 10½ (6.5mm) needles, or size needed to obtain gauge

Size 8 (5mm) circular needle, 16" (40.5cm) long (for neck)

Stitch holders

Stitch markers

Yarn needle

GAUGE

14 stitches and 16 rows = 4" (10cm) in rib stitch, using the larger needles

TAKE TIME TO CHECK GAUGE.

PATTERN STITCHES

K1, P1 Rib
(multiple of 2 stitches)
Round 1 *K1, p1; repeat from * around.
Repeat round 1 for k1, p1 rib.

K3, P3 Rib
(multiple of 6 stitches)
Round 1 *K3, p3; repeat from * around.
Repeat round 1 for k3, p3 rib.

Rib Stitch (multiple of 6 stitches + 1 extra stitch)
Row 1 (right side) K1, p1, *k3, p1, k1, p1; repeat from * across to the last 5 stitches, end k3, p1, k1.
Row 2: Knit the knit stitches and purl the purl stitches as they face you.
Repeat row 2 for rib stitch.

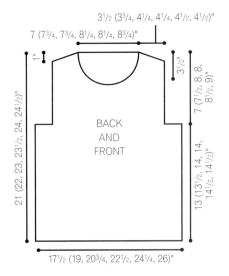

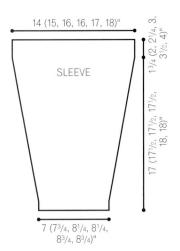

BACK

Cast on 61 (67, 73, 79, 85, 91) stitches.

(Right side) Begin rib stitch; work even until the piece measures 13 (13½, 14, 14, 14½, 14½)" (33 [34.5, 35.5, 35.5, 37, 37]cm) from the beginning, ending with a wrong-side row.

Shape Armhole
(Right side) Bind off 6 (7, 8, 10, 12, 14) stitches at beginning of next 2 rows—49 (53, 57, 59, 61, 63) stitches remain.

Work even until the armhole measures 7 (7½, 8, 8, 8½, 9)" (18 [19, 20.5, 20.5, 21.5, 23]cm) from the shaping, ending with a wrong-side row.

Shape Shoulders and Neck
(Right side) Bind off 6 (6, 7, 7, 8, 8) stitches at beginning of next 2 rows, then 6 (7, 8, 8, 8, 8) stitches at beginning of next 2 rows for the shoulders—25 (27, 27, 29, 29, 31) stitches remain for the neck.

Place the remaining stitches on a holder.

FRONT

Work as for the Back until the armhole measures 4½ (5, 5½, 5½, 6, 6½)" (11.5 [12.5, 14, 14, 15, 16.5]cm) from the shaping, ending with a wrong-side row—49 (53, 57, 59, 61, 63) stitches remain; place a marker at each side of the center 9 (11, 11, 13, 13, 15) stitches.

Shape Neck
(Right side) Work across to the marker; place center stitches on a holder for the neck; join a second ball of yarn, and work to end—20 (21, 23, 23, 24, 24) stitches remain each side. Working both sides at the same time, at each neck edge, bind off 3 stitches once, 2 stitches once, then decrease 1 stitch every other row 3 times—12 (13, 15, 15, 16, 16) stitches remain on each side for the shoulders. Work even until the armhole measures 7 (7½, 8, 8, 8½, 9)" (18 [19, 20.5, 20.5, 21.5, 23]cm) from the shaping, ending with a wrong-side row.

Shape Shoulders
(Right side) Bind off 6 (6, 7, 7, 8, 8) stitches at the beginning of the next 2 rows; 6 (7, 8, 8, 8, 8) stitches at the beginning of the next 2 rows for the shoulders.

SLEEVES (MAKE 2)

Cast on 25 (27, 29, 29, 31, 31) stitches.

Begin Pattern
(Right side) K0 (0, 1, 1, 0, 0), p0 (1, 1, 1, 0, 0); beginning row 1, work rib stitch across 25 (25, 25, 25, 31, 31) stitches, ending p0 (1, 1, 1, 0, 0), k0 (0, 1, 1, 0, 0).

Work even in this way for 6 (4, 8, 8, 8, 6) rows, ending with a wrong-side row.

Shape Sleeve

(Right side) Beginning this row, increase 1 stitch each side every 8 (8, 6, 6, 6, 6) rows 12 (13, 14, 14, 14, 16) times, working increased stitches in pattern—49 (53, 57, 57, 59, 63) stitches.

Work even until the piece measures 17 (17½, 17½, 17½, 18, 18)" (43 [44.5, 44.5, 44.5, 45.5, 45.5]cm) from the beginning; place a marker on each side for the underarm. Work even until the piece measures 1¾ (2, 2¼, 3, 3½, 4)" (4.5 [5, 5.5, 7.5, 9, 10]cm) from the marker.

Bind off all stitches loosely in rib.

FINISHING

If necessary, block the pieces to the measurements, being careful not to flatten the texture.

Turtleneck (Circular Version)

Sew the shoulder seams.

With the right side facing, using the circular needle and beginning at the left shoulder, pick up and knit 60 (60, 60, 66, 66, 66) stitches evenly around the neck shaping, including the stitches on holders; place a marker for the beginning of the round.

Begin k3, p3 rib; work even until the piece measures 5" (12.5cm) from the pickup round.

Change to k1, p1 rib; work even for 1" (2.5cm).

Bind off all stitches loosely in rib.

Turtleneck (Seamed Version)

Sew the right shoulder only.

With the right side facing, using the smaller needle (use the circular needle and work back and forth in rows), beginning at the left shoulder, pick up as for working the circular version, plus 1 extra stitch at each side of the left shoulder for the seam stitches—62 (62, 62, 68, 68, 68) stitches. Keeping the seam stitches in stockinette stitch (knit on the right side, purl on the wrong side), work as for the circular version.

Sew the left shoulder and turtleneck seam.

Set in the Sleeves, matching markers at the underarm shaping; sew the side and sleeve seams.

Using the yarn needle, weave in all ends.

Stornaway Vest

DESIGNED BY NANCY J. THOMAS

Choosing two appropriate colors can be challenging as this simple bicolor vest works as a season-spanning piece. Experiment with which color you plan to use for color A and for color B. Darker shades around the waist and hip area are more flattering.

If crochet isn't your thing, make a quick alternate band by picking up the stitches along the edges and knitting one row and then binding off on the next row. (For a cleaner pickup, work the first row in the color of the piece and change to the contrasting color on the next row.)

EASY

SIZES

X-Small (Small, Medium, Large, 1X, 2X)

KNITTED MEASUREMENTS

Bust 34 (38, 42, 46, 50, 54)" (86 [96.5, 106.5, 117, 127, 137]cm)

Length 18 (19, 19, 20, 20, 20½)" (45.5 [48.5, 48.5, 51, 51, 52]cm)

MATERIALS

3 (3, 4, 4, 4, 5) balls Tahki Yarns New Tweed (60% wool, 26% viscose, 14% silk, 1¾ oz [50g], 92 yd [84m]) in #34 brown (A) and 4 (5, 5, 6, 7, 8) balls in #33 beige (B) (4) medium

Size 7 (4.5mm) and size 8 (5mm) needles, or size needed to obtain gauge

Size G-6 (4mm) crochet hook

Split-ring stitch markers

Yarn needle

5 buttons, 1" (25cm) in diameter

GAUGE

18 stitches and 24 rows = 4" (10cm) in stockinette stitch, using the larger needles

TAKE TIME TO CHECK GAUGE.

PATTERN STITCHES

K2, P2 Rib (multiple of 4 stitches)
Row 1 (wrong side) *K2, p2; repeat from * across.
Row 2 Knit the knit stitches and purl the purl stitches as they face you.
Repeat row 2 for k2, p2 rib.

Stockinette Stitch
Knit on the right side, purl on the wrong side.

Fancy Rib (multiple of 4 stitches + 1 extra stitch)
Row 1 (right side) K1 (edge stitch; keep in stockinette stitch), k3, *p1, k3; repeat from * across to the last stitch, k1 (edge stitch).
Row 2 Purl.
Repeat rows 1 and 2 for fancy rib.

Chain
Wrap the yarn around the crochet hook (yarn over), and draw it through the loop on the hook to form the first chain.

Single Crochet
Insert the crochet hook in the stitch, yarn over and pull up a loop, yarn over and draw through both loops on the hook.

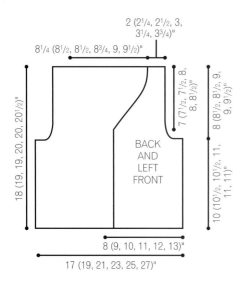

2 (2¼, 2½, 3, 3¼, 3¾)"

8¼ (8½, 8½, 8¾, 9, 9½)"

18 (19, 19, 20, 20½)"

7 (7½, 7½, 8, 8½)"

8 (8½, 8½, 9, 9½)"

BACK AND LEFT FRONT

10 (10½, 10½, 11, 11, 11)"

8 (9, 10, 11, 12, 13)"

17 (19, 21, 23, 25, 27)"

BACK

Using the smaller needles and A, cast on 77 (85, 97, 105, 113, 121) stitches.

(Right side) Begin fancy rib; work even until the piece measures 4" (10cm) from the beginning, increase 0 (1, 0, 0, 0, 0) stitch(es), decrease 0 (0, 2, 1, 0, 0) stitch(es) across the last (wrong-side) row—77 (86, 95, 104, 113, 121) stitches.

(Right side) Change to the larger needles, stockinette stitch, and B; work even until the piece measures 10 (10½, 10½, 11, 11, 11)" (25.5 [26.5, 26.5, 28, 28, 28]cm) from the beginning, ending with a wrong-side row.

Shape Armhole
(Right side) Bind off 3 (3, 4, 5, 6, 7) stitches at the beginning of the next 2 rows, then 2 (4, 5, 6, 7, 7) stitches at the beginning of the next 2 rows—67 (72, 77, 82, 87, 93) stitches remain.

(Right side) Decrease 1 stitch each side every other row 6 (7, 7, 7, 8, 8) times—55 (58, 63, 68, 71, 77) stitches remain.

Work even until the armhole measures 8 (8½, 8½, 9, 9, 9½)" (20.5 [21.5, 21.5, 23, 23, 24]cm) from the beginning of the shaping, ending with a wrong-side row.

Bind off the remaining stitches; place a marker 9 (10, 12, 14, 15, 17) stitches in from each armhole for the shoulders.

LEFT FRONT

Using the smaller needles and A, cast on 37 (41, 45, 49, 53, 57) stitches.

(Right side) Begin fancy rib; work even until the piece measures 4" (10cm) from the beginning, increase 0 (0, 0, 1, 1, 2) stitch(es), decrease 1 (0, 0, 0, 0, 0) stitch(es) across the last (wrong-side) row—36 (41, 45, 50, 54, 59) stitches.

(Right side) Change to the larger needles, stockinette stitch, and B; work even until the piece measures 10 (10½, 10½, 11, 11, 11)" (25.5 [26.5, 26.5, 28, 28, 28]cm) from the beginning, ending with a wrong-side row.

Shape Armhole
(Right side) At the armhole edge, bind off 3 (3, 4, 5, 6, 7) stitches once, then 2 (4, 5, 6, 7, 7) stitches once—31 (34, 36, 39, 41, 45) stitches remain.

(Right side) At the armhole edge, decrease 1 stitch every other row 6 (7, 7, 7, 8, 8) times, and AT THE SAME TIME, when the armhole measures 1" (2.5cm) from the beginning of the shaping, end with a wrong-side row.

Shape Neck
(Right side) Continuing the armhole shaping at the beginning of the right-side rows, work across to the last 3 stitches, ssk, k1 (edge stitch).

(Right side) At the neck edge, decrease 1 stitch every other row 15 (16, 16, 17, 17, 19) times—9 (10, 12, 14, 15, 17) stitches remain for the shoulder.

Work even until the armhole measures 8 (8½, 8½, 9, 9, 9½)" (20.5 [21.5, 21.5, 23, 23, 24]cm) from the beginning of the shaping.

Bind off the remaining stitches.

RIGHT FRONT

Work as for the left Front until the piece measures 10 (10½, 10½, 11, 11, 11)" (25.5 [26.5, 26.5, 28, 28, 28]cm) from the beginning, ending with a right-side row—36 (41, 45, 50, 54, 59) stitches.

Shape Armhole

(Wrong side) At the armhole edge, bind off 3 (3, 4, 5, 6, 7) stitches once, then 2 (4, 5, 6, 7, 7) stitches once—31 (34, 36, 39, 41, 45) stitches remain. Work 1 row even.

(Right side) At the armhole edge (the end of the right-side rows), decrease 1 stitch every other row 6 (7, 7, 7, 8, 8) times, and AT THE SAME TIME, when the armhole measures 1" (2.5cm) from the beginning of the shaping, end with a wrong-side row.

Shape Neck

(Right side) At the neck edge (the beginning of the right-side rows), k1 (edge stitch), k2tog, work to end, continuing the armhole shaping.

(Right side) At the neck edge, decrease 1 stitch every other row 15 (16, 16, 17, 17, 19) times—9 (10, 12, 14, 15, 17) stitches remain for the shoulder.

Work even until the armhole measures 8 (8½, 8½, 9, 9, 9½)" (20.5 [21.5, 21.5, 23, 23, 24]cm) from the beginning of the shaping.

Bind off the remaining stitches.

FINISHING

Block the pieces to the measurements. Sew the shoulder seams. Sew the side seams.

Left Front Band

With the right side facing, using the smaller needles and A and beginning at the neck edge, pick up and knit 58 (62, 62, 66, 66, 70) stitches down the left Front to the lower edge.

(Wrong side) Begin k2, p2 rib, beginning p2; work even for 8 rows.

Bind off all stitches loosely in rib.

Button Loops

Place markers for the 5 button loops, evenly spaced along the right Front edge, with the first one 1" (2.5cm) from the lower edge, the last one ½" (13mm) from the beginning of the neck shaping, and the remaining 3 evenly spaced between.

With the right side facing, using the crochet hook and B, join the yarn with a slip stitch at the lower right Front.

Row 1 Chain 1, single crochet evenly up the right Front to the neck edge, turn.

Row 2 Chain 1, single crochet in each single crochet to first marker, *[chain 3, skip 3 single crochet for the button loop], single crochet in each single crochet to the next marker; repeat from * for the remaining button loops, single crochet to end.

Fasten off.

Neck Edging

With the right side facing, using the crochet hook and A, join the yarn with a slip stitch at the right Front neck edge.

Work 2 rows single crochet evenly around the neck shaping, ending at the left neck edge above the Front band on the first row.

Fasten off.

Armhole Edging

With the right side facing, using the crochet hook and A, join the yarn with a slip stitch at the underarm seam.

Work 2 rows single crochet evenly around the armhole; join with a slip stitch to the first stitch.

Fasten off.

Using the yarn needle, weave in all ends. Sew on the buttons opposite the button loops.

Galway Tie-Front Cardigan

DESIGNED BY NANCY J. THOMAS

Is it a vest, a sweater, or a combination of the two? Using two shades of a tweedy-looking yarn, you will have the best of both in this easy-to-make, relaxed-look cardigan with front pockets. Instead of buttons, skinny ribbed ties make a distinctive center front. The knit 2, purl 2 rib creates stretchy sleeves that move with you. With no bands and buttonholes, this project is a perfect first cardigan to knit—and it's available in five sizes!

EASY

SIZES

Small (Medium, Large, 1X, 2X)

KNITTED MEASUREMENTS

Bust 37 (41, 45, 49, 53)" (94 [104, 114, 124.5, 134.5]cm)

Length 21 (22, 22½, 23, 23½)" (53.5 [56, 57, 58.5, 59.5]cm)

MATERIALS

4 (5, 6, 6, 7) balls Tahki Yarns Shannon (100% wool, 1¾ oz [50g], 92 yd [84m]) in #14 red mix (MC) and 2 (2, 2, 3, 3) balls in #18 rose multi (CC) (4) medium

Size 6 (4mm) and size 7 (4.5mm) needles, or size needed to obtain gauge

Size 6 (4 mm) circular needle, 36" (91cm) long, for Front band

Stitch holders

Stitch markers

Yarn needle

GAUGE

16 stitches and 22 rows = 4" (10cm) in stockinette stitch, using the larger needles

TAKE TIME TO CHECK GAUGE.

PATTERN STITCHES

Garter Stitch
Knit every row.

Stockinette Stitch
Knit on the right side, purl on the wrong side.

K2, P2 Rib
(multiple of 4 stitches +
2 extra stitches)
Row 1 (right side) K2, *p2, k2;
repeat from * across.
Row 2 Knit the knit stitches and purl the purl stitches as they face you.
Repeat row 2 for k2, p2 rib.

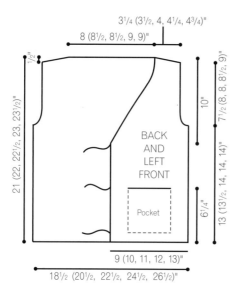

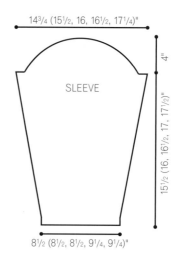

BACK

Using the smaller needles and MC, cast on 74 (82, 90, 98, 106) stitches.

(Right side) Begin garter stitch; work even for 4 rows, ending with a wrong-side row.

(Right side) Change to the larger needles and stockinette stitch; work even until the piece measures 13 (13½, 14, 14, 14)" (33 [34.5, 35.5, 35.5, 35.5]cm) from the beginning, ending with a wrong-side row.

Shape Armhole
(Right side) Bind off 3 (4, 4, 4, 5) stitches at the beginning of the next 2 rows, then 2 (3, 4, 5, 5) stitches at the beginning of the next 2 rows—64 (68, 74, 80, 86) stitches remain.

(Right side) Decrease 1 stitch each side every other row 3 (3, 4, 5, 6) times—58 (62, 66, 70, 74) stitches remain. Work even until the armhole measures 7½ (8, 8, 8½, 9)" (19 [20.5, 20.5, 21.5, 23]cm) from the beginning of the shaping, ending with a wrong-side row.

Shape Shoulders and Neck
(Right side) Bind off 13 (14, 16, 17, 19) stitches at the beginning of the next 2 rows—32 (34, 34, 36, 36) stitches remain for the neck.

Bind off the remaining stitches.

POCKET LINING (MAKE 2)

Using the larger needles, cast on 20 stitches.

(Right side) Begin stockinette stitch; work even until the piece measures 5¾" (14.5cm) from the beginning.

Place the stitches on a holder.

LEFT FRONT

Using the smaller needles and MC, cast on 36 (40, 44, 48, 52) stitches.

(Right side) Begin garter stitch; work even for 4 rows, ending with a wrong-side row.

(Right side) Change to the larger needles and stockinette stitch; work even until the piece measures 6¼" (16cm) from the beginning, ending with a wrong-side row.

Insert Pocket Lining
(Right side) Work across 8 (10, 12, 14, 16) stitches; place the next 20 stitches on a holder for the Pocket edge; with the right side of the Pocket Lining facing, knit across the stitches on the holder; work to end.

(Wrong side) Continuing in stockinette stitch, work even until the piece measures 11 (12, 12½, 13, 13½)" (28 [30.5, 32, 33, 34.5]cm) from the beginning, ending with a right-side row.

Shape Neck

(Wrong side) At the neck edge, decrease 1 stitch [alternately every other row and then every 4 rows] 7 (6, 6, 6, 6) times, then every other row 1 (4, 4, 5, 5) time(s); AT THE SAME TIME, when the piece measures 13 (13½, 14, 14, 14)" (33 [34.5, 35.5, 35.5, 35.5]cm) from the beginning, end with a wrong-side row.

Shape Armhole

(Right side) At the armhole edge, bind off 3 (4, 4, 4, 5) stitches once, then 2 (3, 4, 5, 5) stitches once.

(Right side) At the armhole edge, decrease 1 stitch every other row 3 (3, 4, 5, 6) times—13 (14, 16, 17, 19) stitches remain for the shoulder when the neck shaping is completed. Work even until the armhole measures 7½ (8, 8, 8½, 9)" (19 [20.5, 20.5, 21.5, 23]cm) from the beginning of the shaping, ending with a wrong-side row.

Shape Shoulder

(Right side) Bind off the remaining stitches.

RIGHT FRONT

Using the smaller needles and MC, cast on 36 (40, 44, 48, 52) stitches.

(Right side) Begin garter stitch; work even for 4 rows, ending with a wrong-side row.

(Right side) Change to the larger needles and stockinette stitch; work even until the piece measures 6¼" (16cm) from the beginning, ending with a wrong-side row.

Insert Pocket Lining

(Right side) Work across 8 (10, 12, 14, 16) stitches; place the next 20 stitches on a holder for the Pocket edge; with the right side of the Pocket Lining facing, knit across the stitches on the holder; work to end.

(Wrong side) Continuing in stockinette stitch, work even until the piece measures 11 (12, 12½, 13, 13½)" (28 [30.5, 32, 33, 34.5]cm) from the beginning, ending with a wrong-side row.

Shape Neck

(Right side) At the neck edge, decrease 1 stitch [alternately every other row and then every 4 rows] 7 (6, 6, 6, 6) times, then every other row 1 (4, 4, 5, 5) time(s); AT THE SAME TIME, when the piece measures 13 (13½, 14, 14, 14)" (33 [34.5, 35.5, 35.5, 35.5]cm) from the beginning, end with a right-side row.

Shape Armhole

(Wrong side) At the armhole edge, bind off 3 (4, 4, 4, 5) stitches once, then 2 (3, 4, 5, 5) stitches once.

(Wrong side) At the armhole edge, decrease 1 stitch every other row 3 (3, 4, 5, 6) times—13 (14, 16, 17, 19) stitches remain for the shoulder when the neck shaping is completed. Work even until the armhole measures 7½ (8, 8, 8½, 9)" (19 [20.5, 20.5, 21.5, 23]cm) from the beginning of the shaping, ending with a right-side row.

Shape Shoulder

(Wrong side) Bind off the remaining stitches.

SLEEVES (MAKE 2)

Using the smaller needles and CC, cast on 42 (42, 42, 46, 46) stitches.

(Right side) Begin k2, p2 rib, end k2; work even for 6 (6, 6, 6, 4) rows, ending with a wrong-side row.

Shape Sleeve

(Right side) Beginning this row, increase 1 stitch each side [alternately every 4 rows, then every 6 rows] 8 times, then every 4 rows 0 (2, 3, 2, 4) times, working the increased stitches in rib as they become available—74 (78, 80, 82, 86) stitches.

Work even until the piece measures 15½ (16, 16½, 17, 17½)" (39.5 [40.5, 42, 43, 44.5]cm) from the beginning, ending with a wrong-side row.

Shape Cap

(Right side) Bind off 3 (4, 4, 4, 5) stitches at the beginning of the next 2 rows, then 2 (3, 4, 5, 5) stitches at the beginning of the next 2 rows—64 (64, 64, 64, 66) stitches remain.

(Right side) Decrease 1 stitch each side every other row 6 times—52 (52, 52, 52, 54) stitches remain.

(Right side) Bind off 3 stitches at the beginning of the next 2 rows, then 4 stitches at the beginning of the next 6 rows—22 (22, 22, 22, 24) stitches remain.

Bind off the remaining stitches.

TIES (MAKE 6)

Using the larger needles and MC, cast on 4 stitches.

(Right side) Begin k2, p2 rib.

Work even until the piece measures 5" (12.5cm) from the beginning.

Place the stitches on a holder.

FINISHING

Block the pieces to the measurements. Sew the shoulder seams.

Front Band and Ties

Place markers for 3 Ties, evenly spaced on both Fronts, with the first one 1½" (4cm) from the lower edge, the last one 1½" (4cm) from the beginning of the neck shaping, and the remaining one centered between.

With the right side facing, using the circular needle and MC and beginning at the lower right Front, pick up and knit 6 (5, 5, 6, 6) stitches to the first marker; *pick up and knit 4 stitches, working the stitches of one Tie together with 4 picked-up stitches; pick up and knit 12 (14, 15, 16, 17) stitches to the next marker*; repeat from * to * once, pick up and knit 4 stitches, working stitches together with Tie, pick up and knit 2 stitches to the beginning of the neck shaping; pick up and knit 45 stitches along the right Front neck shaping to the shoulder, 32 (34, 34, 36, 36) stitches across the Back neck, 45 stitches along the left Front neck shaping; pick up and knit 2 stitches down the left Front; repeat from * to * twice, pick up and knit 4 stitches, working the stitches together with the Tie, pick up and knit 6 (5, 5, 6, 6) stitches to the lower left Front—210 (218, 222, 230, 234) stitches.

(Wrong side) Begin k2, p2 rib, end k2; work even until the band measures 1½" (4cm) from the pickup row.

Bind off all stitches loosely in rib.

Pocket Bands

With the right side facing, using the smaller needles, place the stitches from the Pocket on the needle, ready to work a wrong-side row.

(Wrong side) P2tog, p1, work k2, p2 rib across the center 12 stitches, end k2, p1, p2tog.

Continue in k2, p2 rib for 7 rows, ending with a wrong-side row.

Bind off all stitches loosely in rib. Sew the Band ends in place.

Set in the Sleeves, matching the shaping; sew the side and sleeve seams.

Using the yarn needle, weave in all ends.

Chapter 6

WALKING THE IRISH CLIFFS OF MOHER

Projects for Intermediate Knitters

Cables are especially important to the sweaters in this chapter. Three of the projects are rich with cables, from easy twists to more involved ones. All the cable patterns include both words and charts. Use the method you find easiest. Stitch markers are essential for cabled projects.

Along with cables, it's time to create some unique fabrics by exploring knit- and purl-stitch patterns. As an intermediate knitter, you'll also learn how to increase and decrease in pattern. It's a good idea to find a method for keeping track of your progress along the way. Simple tick marks can work as well as a row counter.

Moss Cabled Cardigan

DESIGNED BY NANCY J. THOMAS

For texture and style, homespun-style tweed yarn and cables are a perfect combination. The stitch definition of the cables and the textural knit 2, purl 2 ribbing is superb. Lots of buttons keep the bands from gapping open.

This cardigan, with its three simple cable panels on the back and one panel each on all the other pieces, is a snap to knit. Once you have the back, fronts, and sleeves assembled, make the knit 2, purl 2 ribbing collar and bands. Then sew on the buttons, and you're done.

INTERMEDIATE

SIZES

Small (Medium, Large, 1X, 2X)

KNITTED MEASUREMENTS

Bust 34 (38, 42, 46, 50)" (86 [96.5, 106.5, 117, 127]cm)

Length 22 (22½, 23, 23½, 24)" (56 [57, 58.5, 59.5, 61]cm)

MATERIALS

6 (7, 7, 8, 9) balls Tahki Yarns Donegal Tweed (100% pure new wool, 3½ oz [100g], 183 yd [167m]) in #892 green (4) medium

Size 6 (4mm) and size 8 (5mm) needles, or size needed to obtain gauge

Stitch markers

Cable needle

Stitch holders

Yarn needle

9 buttons, 1" (25mm) in diameter

GAUGE

18 stitches and 24 rows = 4" (10cm) in stockinette stitch, using the larger needles

TAKE TIME TO CHECK GAUGE.

ABBREVIATIONS AND TERMS

C6B Slip 3 stitches onto a cable needle and hold to the back, knit 3 stitches, knit 3 stitches from the cable needle.

C6F Slip 3 stitches onto a cable needle and hold to the front, knit 3 stitches, knit 3 stitches from the cable needle.

PATTERN STITCHES

K2, P2 Rib (multiple of 4 stitches + 2 extra stitches)
Row 1 (right side) K2, *p2, k2; repeat from * across.
Row 2 Knit the knit stitches and purl the purl stitches as they face you. Repeat row 2 for k2, p2 rib.

Stockinette Stitch
Knit on the right side, purl on the wrong side.

Garter Stitch
Knit every row.

Cable (panel of 15 stitches; see chart)
Rows 1 and 3 (right side) P1, k6, p1, k6, p1.
Row 2 and all wrong-side rows Knit the knit stitches and purl the purl stitches as they face you.
Row 5 P1, C6B, p1, C6F, p1.
Rows 7–8 Repeat rows 1 and 2.
Repeat rows 1–8 for cable.

Note: When working the armhole and neck shaping, work decreases 1 stitch in from the edge.

CABLE CHART

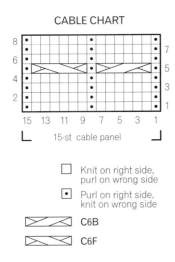

15-st cable panel

☐ Knit on right side, purl on wrong side

⊡ Purl on right side, knit on wrong side

▱ C6B

▱ C6F

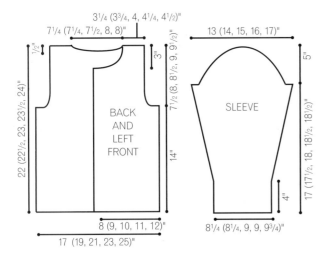

3¼ (3¾, 4, 4¼, 4½)"
7¼ (7¼, 7½, 8, 8)"
½"
3"
7½ (8, 8½, 9, 9½)"
22 (22½, 23, 23½, 24)"
14"
BACK AND LEFT FRONT
8 (9, 10, 11, 12)"
17 (19, 21, 23, 25)"

13 (14, 15, 16, 17)"
5"
SLEEVE
17 (17½, 18, 18½, 18½)"
4"
8¼ (8¼, 9, 9, 9¾)"

BACK

Using the smaller needles, cast on 90 (98, 110, 118, 130) stitches.

(Right side) Begin k2, p2 rib, end k2; work even until the piece measures 3½" (9cm) from the beginning, decrease 1 (0, 1, 0, 1) stitch(es), increase 0 (1, 0, 1, 0) stitch(es) across the last (wrong-side) row—89 (99, 109, 119, 129) stitches remain.

Change to the larger needles.

Begin Pattern
(Right side) K10 (13, 16, 19, 22), place a marker; beginning row 1, work cable across the next 15 stitches, place a marker; *k12 (14, 16, 18, 20), place a marker; work cable across the next 15 stitches, place a marker; repeat from * once more, knit the remaining 10 (13, 16, 19, 22) stitches.

Continue in this way, working the stitches on each side of the cables in stockinette stitch for 5 more rows, ending with a wrong-side row.

Shape Body
(Right side) Beginning this row, decrease 1 stitch each side every 6 rows 4 times—81 (91, 101, 111, 121) stitches remain.

Work even until the piece measures 9½" (24cm) from the beginning, ending with a wrong-side row.

(Right side) Beginning this row, increase 1 stitch each side every 8 rows 3 times—87 (97, 107, 117, 127) stitches. Work even in pattern until the piece measures 14" (35.5cm) from the beginning, ending with a wrong-side row.

Shape Armhole
(Right side) Bind off 3 (4, 5, 6, 7) stitches at the beginning of the next 2 rows, then 2 (3, 4, 5, 6) stitches at the beginning of the next 2 rows—77 (83, 89, 95, 101) stitches remain.

(Right side) Decrease 1 stitch each side every other row 3 (4, 5, 6, 7) times—71 (75, 79, 83, 87) stitches remain. Work even until the armhole measures 7 (7½, 8, 8½, 9)" (18 [19, 20.5, 21.5, 23]cm) from the beginning of the shaping, ending with a wrong-side row; place a marker each side of the center 29 (29, 31, 33, 33) stitches.

Shape Neck and Shoulders

(Right side) Work across to the marker; place center stitches on a holder for the neck; join a second ball of yarn and work to end.

Working both sides at the same time, at each neck edge bind off 2 stitches twice—17 (19, 20, 21, 23) stitches remain each shoulder.

Bind off the remaining stitches at the beginning of the next 2 rows.

LEFT FRONT

Using the smaller needles, cast on 43 (47, 51, 55, 63) stitches.

(Right side) Begin k2, p2 rib, ending k2, k1 (edge stitch; keep in garter stitch throughout) at the center Front.

Continue in this way, working 1 stitch in garter stitch at the center Front and the remaining stitches in k2, p2 rib, until the piece measures 3½" (9cm) from the beginning, decrease 2 (1, 0, 0, 2) stitch(es), increase 0 (0, 0, 1, 0) stitch(es) evenly across the last (wrong-side) row—41 (46, 51, 56, 61) stitches remain.

Change to the larger needles.

Begin Pattern

(Right side) K10 (13, 16, 19, 22), place a marker; beginning row 1, work cable across the next 15 stitches, place a marker; k15 (17, 19, 21, 23), k1 (edge stitch).

Continue in this way, maintaining the edge stitch at the center Front, working stitches on each side of the cable in stockinette stitch for 5 more rows, ending with a wrong-side row.

Shape Body

(Right side) Beginning this row, at the armhole edge, decrease 1 stitch every 6 rows 4 times—37 (42, 47, 52, 57) stitches remain.

Work even until the piece measures 9½" (24cm) from the beginning, ending with a wrong-side row.

(Right side) Beginning this row, at the armhole edge, increase 1 stitch every 8 rows 3 times—40 (45, 50, 55, 60) stitches. Work even in pattern until the piece measures 14" (35.5cm) from the beginning, ending with a wrong-side row.

Shape Armhole

(Right side) At the armhole edge, bind off 3 (4, 5, 6, 7) stitches once, then 2 (3, 4, 5, 6) stitches once—35 (38, 41, 44, 47) stitches remain.

(Right side) Decrease 1 stitch each side every other row 3 (4, 5, 6, 7) times—32 (34, 36, 38, 40) stitches remain.

Work even until the armhole measures 4½ (5, 5½, 6, 6½)" (11.5 [12.5, 14, 15, 16.5]cm) from the beginning of the shaping, ending with a wrong-side row.

Shape Neck and Shoulders

(Right side) Work across to the last 5 (5, 6, 7, 7) stitches; place the remaining stitches on a holder for the neck; turn—27 (29, 30, 31, 33) stitches remain.

(Wrong side) At the neck edge, bind off 2 stitches every other row 3 times, then decrease 1 stitch every other row 4 times—17 (19, 20, 21, 23) stitches remain for the shoulder.

Work even until the armhole measures 7½ (8, 8½, 9, 9½)" (19 [20.5, 21.5, 23, 24]cm) from the beginning of the shaping, ending with a wrong-side row.

Bind off the remaining stitches.

RIGHT FRONT

Using the smaller needles, cast on 43 (47, 51, 55, 63) stitches.

(Right side) K1 (edge stitch), begin k2, p2 rib, ending k2 at the armhole edge.

Continue in this way, working 1 stitch in garter stitch at the center Front and the remaining stitches in k2, p2 rib, until the piece measures 3½" (9cm) from the beginning, decrease 2 (1, 0, 0, 2) stitch(es), increase 0 (0, 0, 1, 0) stitch(es) evenly across the last (wrong-side) row—41 (46, 51, 56, 61) stitches remain.

Begin Pattern

(Right side) K1 (edge stitch), k15 (17, 19, 21, 23), place a marker; beginning row 1, work cable across the next 15 stitches, place a marker; k10 (13, 16, 19, 22).

Continue in this way, maintaining the edge stitch at the center Front and working stitches each side of the cable in stockinette stitch for 5 rows, ending with a right-side row.

Shape Body

(Wrong side) Beginning this row, at the armhole edge, decrease 1 stitch every 6 rows 4 times—37 (42, 47, 52, 57) stitches remain.

Work even until the piece measures 9½" (24cm) from the beginning, ending with a right-side row.

(Wrong side) Beginning this row, at the armhole edge, increase 1 stitch every 8 rows 3 times—40 (45, 50, 55, 60) stitches. Work even in pattern until the piece measures 14" (35.5cm) from the beginning, ending with a right-side row.

Shape Armhole

(Wrong side) At the armhole edge, bind off 3 (4, 5, 6, 7) stitches once, then 2 (3, 4, 5, 6) stitches once—35 (38, 41, 44, 47) stitches remain.

(Wrong side) Decrease 1 stitch each side every other row 3 (4, 5, 6, 7) times—32 (34, 36, 38, 40) stitches remain.

Work even until the armhole measures 4½ (5, 5½, 6, 6½)" (11.5 [12.5, 14, 15, 16.5]cm) from the beginning of the shaping, ending with a wrong-side row.

Shape Neck and Shoulders

(Right side) Work across 5 (5, 6, 7, 7) stitches, place on a holder for the neck; work to end—27 (29, 30, 31, 33) stitches remain.

(Right side) At the neck edge, bind off 2 stitches every other row 3 times, then decrease 1 stitch every other row 4 times—17 (19, 20, 21, 23) stitches remain for the shoulder.

Work even until the armhole measures 7½ (8, 8½, 9, 9½)" (19 [20.5, 21.5, 23, 24]cm) from the beginning of the shaping, ending with a right-side row.

Bind off the remaining stitches.

SLEEVES (MAKE 2)

Using the smaller needles, cast on 46 (46, 50, 50, 54) stitches.

(Right side) Begin k2, p2 rib, end k2; work even until the piece measures 4" (10cm) from the beginning, decreasing 1 stitch across the last (wrong-side) row— 45 (45, 49, 49, 53) stitches remain.

Change to the larger needles.

Begin Pattern
(Right side) K15 (15, 17, 17, 19), place a marker; beginning row 1, work cable across the next 15 stitches, place a marker; k15 (15, 17, 17, 19).

Continue in this way, working stitches on each side of the cable in stockinette stitch for 3 rows, ending with a wrong-side row.

Shape Sleeve
(Right side) Continuing in pattern, beginning this row, increase 1 stitch each side every 6 rows 0 (2, 1, 13, 13) times, every 8 rows 2 (8, 9, 0, 0) times, every 10 rows 6 (0, 0, 0, 0) times, working increased stitches in stockinette stitch—61 (65, 69, 75, 79) stitches.

Work even until the piece measures 17 (17½, 18, 18½, 18½)" (43 [44.5, 45.5, 47, 47]cm) from the beginning, ending with a wrong-side row.

Shape Cap
(Right side) Bind off 3 (4, 5, 6, 7) stitches at beginning of next 2 rows, then 2 (3, 4, 5, 6) stitches at beginning of next 2 rows—51 (51, 51, 53, 53) stitches remain.

(Right side) Decrease 1 stitch each side every other row 7 times—37 (37, 37, 39, 39) stitches remain.

(Right side) Bind off 2 stitches at beginning of next 10 rows—17 (17, 17, 19, 19) stitches remain.

(Right side) Bind off 3 (3, 3, 4, 4) stitches at beginning of next 2 rows—11 stitches remain.

Bind off the remaining stitches.

FINISHING

Block the pieces to the measurements, being careful not to flatten the texture. Sew the shoulder seams.

Collar
With the right side facing, using the smaller needles, pick up and knit 98 (98, 102, 106, 106) stitches evenly around the neck shaping, including the stitches on holders.

(Wrong side) Begin k2, p2 rib, end k2; work even until the collar measures 5" (12.5cm) from the pickup row.

Bind off all stitches loosely in pattern.

Button Band
With the right side facing, using the smaller needles and beginning at the upper edge of the collar, pick up and knit 130 (134, 134, 138, 138) stitches along the left Front to the lower edge.

(Wrong side) Begin k2, p2 rib, end k2; work even for 8 rows.

Bind off all stitches loosely in pattern.

Buttonhole Band
Place markers for 9 buttonholes along the right Front edge, with the first one 1" (2.5cm) from the lower edge, the last one 1" (2.5cm) from the upper edge of the collar, and the remaining 7 evenly spaced between.

With the right side facing, using the smaller needles and beginning at the lower edge, pick up and knit 130 (134, 134, 138, 138) stitches along the right Front to the upper edge of the collar.

(Wrong side) Begin k2, p2 rib, end k2; work even for 3 rows, ending with a wrong-side row.

Buttonhole Row *Work in pattern to the marker, [k2tog, yarn over for buttonhole]; repeat from * for the remaining buttonholes, working to the end.

Complete as for the Button Band.

Set in the Sleeves; sew the side and sleeve seams.

Using the yarn needle, weave in all ends. Sew on the buttons opposite the buttonholes.

Scottish Isles Pullover

DESIGNED BY NANCY J. THOMAS

You'll feel like an Irish or Scottish country lass when you pair rustic tweed-fabric skirts with this fitted-cabled pullover. The flow of this shaped sweater lends a feminine touch to a classic, simple design, while the placket and collar add a contemporary look to this otherwise standard crew pullover.

The eight-row cable is simple, making this a very approachable project. Keep track of the shaping by marking off rows as you knit.

INTERMEDIATE

SIZES

Small (Medium, Large, X-Large)

KNITTED MEASUREMENTS

Bust 36 (40, 44, 48)" (91 [101.5, 112, 122]cm)

Length 22 (22½, 23, 23½)" (56 [57, 58.5, 59.5]cm)

Note: The stitch pattern is stretchy; the widths are approximate.

MATERIALS

6 (7, 8, 9) skeins Tahki Yarns Donegal Tweed (100% pure new wool, 3½ oz [100g], 183 yd [167m]) in #863 red **(4)** medium

Size 7 (4.5mm) needles, or size needed to obtain gauge

Cable needle

Stitch markers

Stitch holders

Yarn needle

GAUGE

20 stitches and 25 rows = 4" (10cm) in reverse stockinette stitch

TAKE TIME TO CHECK GAUGE.

ABBREVIATIONS AND TERMS

C6B Slip 3 stitches onto a cable needle, hold to the back, knit 3 stitches, knit 3 stitches from the cable needle.

M1 (Make 1 increase) Lift the strand between the needles to the left-hand needle and work the strand through the back loop, twisting it to prevent a hole, [knit or purl as indicated by pattern stitch].

Tw2L Skip the first stitch on the left-hand needle; knit the next stitch through the back loop, leaving the stitch on left-hand needle; knit the skipped stitch through the front loop; slip both stitches off the left-hand needle.

Tw2R Knit 2 stitches together, leaving the stitches on the left-hand needle; knit the first stitch again; slip both stitches off the left-hand needle.

PATTERN STITCHES

Reverse Stockinette Stitch
Purl on the right side, knit on the wrong side.

Cable
(panel of 6 stitches; see chart)
Row 1 (right side) Knit.
Row 2 and all wrong-side rows Purl.
Row 3 C6B.
Rows 5 and 7 Knit.
Row 8 Repeat row 2.
Repeat rows 1–8 for cable.

C6B CABLE

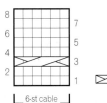

□ Knit on right side, purl on wrong side

⧅ C6B

6-st cable

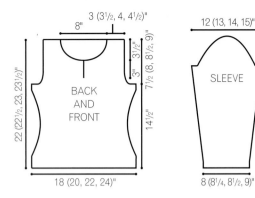

BACK

Cast on 106 (116, 126, 136) stitches.

Begin Cable Rib Pattern
Note: In the following instructions, each k6 in row 1 = row 1 of a cable; all purl stitches in row 1 should be worked in reverse stockinette stitch throughout.

Row 1 (right side) P7 (9, 11, 13), place a marker; [k6, p9 (10, 11, 12), place a marker] twice; [k6, p7 (8, 9, 10)] twice; [k6, place a marker, p9 (10, 11, 12)] twice; k6, place a marker, p7 (9, 11, 13).

Row 2 Knit the knit stitches and purl the purl stitches as they face you.

Row 3 Purl the purl stitches as they face you; work row 3 of cable (C6B) across each cable.

Rows 4–10 Continue in pattern, working the wrong-side rows as row 2 and the right-side rows as row 1, slipping the markers.

Shape Body
***Decrease Row** Work as for row 3 and, AT THE SAME TIME, [work across to 2 stitches before the marker, p2tog] 3 times, [work across to the next marker, p2tog] 3 times, work to end.

Note: At the beginning of the row, decreases are worked on the 2 stitches before the first, second, and third cables; at the end of the row, decreases are worked after the fifth, sixth, and seventh cables—100 (110, 120, 130) stitches remain.

Continuing in pattern, work even for 7 rows.

Repeat from * twice, then work a decrease row once more—82 (92, 102, 112) stitches remain; mark the last decrease row.

Continuing in pattern, work even until the piece measures 3" (7.5cm) from the marker (last decrease row), ending after working row 2 of the cable rib pattern.

***Increase Row** Work as for row 3 and, AT THE SAME TIME, [work across to the marker, M1, slip the marker] 3 times; [work across to the next marker, slip the marker, M1] 3 times, work to end.

Note: Increases are made at the same points where decreases were made previously.

Continuing in pattern, work 7 rows even.

Repeat from * twice, then work the increase row once more—106 (116, 126, 136) stitches.

Work even until the piece measures 14½" (37cm) from the beginning, or the desired length to the underarm, ending with a wrong-side row.

Shape Armhole
(Right side) Bind off 4 (5, 6, 7) stitches at the beginning of the next 2 rows—98 (106, 114, 122) stitches remain.

(Right side) Decrease 1 stitch each side every row 6 times, then every other row 2 (3, 4, 5) times—82 (88, 94, 100) stitches remain. Work even until the armhole measures 7½ (8, 8½, 9)" (19 [20.5, 21.5, 23]cm) from the beginning of the shaping, ending with a wrong-side row.

Shape Shoulders and Neck
(Right side) Bind off 19 (22, 25, 28) stitches at beginning of next 2 rows for the shoulders—44 stitches remain for the neck.

Place the remaining stitches on a holder.

FRONT

Work as for the Back until the piece measures 14½" (37cm) from the beginning, or the desired length to the underarm, ending with a wrong-side row—106 (116, 126, 136) stitches.

Shape Armhole
(Right side) Shape the armhole as for the Back, and AT THE SAME TIME, when the armhole measures 1 (1½, 2, 2½)" (2.5 [3.8, 5, 6.5]cm) from the beginning of the shaping, end with a wrong-side row.

Shape Neck Opening
(Right side) Work in pattern across to the 6-stitch center cable; work [(Tw2R) twice, Tw2L] across the cable, work in pattern to the end.

Dividing Row (wrong side) Work across to 6 stitches of the same center cable; p2, k1 for the right Front; join a second ball of yarn, k1, p2, work to the end for the left Front.

Left Front (right side) Work in pattern across to 3 stitches before the opening; Tw2R, k1 (keep in garter stitch throughout).

Right Front (right side) K1 (keep in garter stitch throughout), Tw2L, work in pattern to the end.

Continue in this way, working both sides at the same time and completing armhole shaping, until the piece measures 3" (7.5cm) from the beginning of the opening, ending with a wrong-side row—41 (44, 47, 50) stitches remain on each side after the armhole shaping is completed.

Shape Neck

Left Front Work in pattern across to the last 12 stitches, place the remaining stitches on a holder.

Right Front Work 12 stitches, place on a holder, work to end in pattern.

Working both sides at the same time, at each neck edge decrease 1 stitch every other row 4 times, then every row 4 times, then every other row 2 times—19 (22, 25, 28) stitches remain each shoulder.

Work even until the armhole measures the same as the Back to the shoulder. Bind off the remaining stitches.

SLEEVES (MAKE 2)

Cast on 46 (48, 50, 52) stitches.

Begin Pattern

Note: In the following instructions, each k6 in row 1 = row 1 of a cable; all purl stitches in row 1 should be worked in reverse stockinette stitch throughout.

Row 1 (right side) P5 (6, 7, 8), [k6, p9] twice, k6, p5 (6, 7, 8).

Row 2 Knit the knit stitches and purl the purl stitches as they face you.

Row 3 Purl the purl stitches as they face you; work row 3 of cable (C6B) across each cable.

Continue in pattern, working the cable every 8 rows; work even for 7 rows, ending with a wrong-side row.

Shape Sleeve

(Right side) Continue in pattern; beginning this row, increase 1 stitch each side every 8 (8, 8, 7) rows 10 (12, 13, 15) times, working increased stitches in reverse stockinette stitch as they become available—66 (72, 76, 82) stitches.

Work even until the piece measures 17 (17½, 18, 18½)" (43 [44.5, 45.5, 47]cm) from the beginning, ending with a wrong-side row.

Shape Cap

(Right side) Bind off 4 (5, 6, 7) stitches at the beginning of the next 2 rows—58 (62, 64, 68) stitches remain.

(Right side) Decrease 1 stitch each side every row 6 times—46 (50, 52, 56) stitches remain.

(Right side) Decrease 1 stitch each side every other row 12 times—22 (26, 28, 32) stitches remain.

(Right side) Bind off 3 (4, 4, 5) stitches at the beginning of the next 4 rows—10 (10, 12, 12) stitches remain.

Bind off the remaining stitches.

FINISHING

Block the pieces to the measurements, being careful not to flatten the texture. Sew the shoulder seams. Set in the Sleeves; sew the side and sleeve seams.

Collar

With the right side facing, pick up and knit 82 stitches around the neck shaping, including the stitches on the holders.

Note: Adjust the pickup number slightly, if necessary, to continue the pattern of cables and reverse stockinette stitch from the stitches on the holders, and to work a 6-stitch cable at each shoulder seam.

(Wrong side) Begin cable and rib pattern as on the Back and Front on all stitches, adjusting the number of stitches in reverse stockinette stitch between cables as necessary on the picked-up stitches between the holders; work even until the collar measures 3" (7.5cm) from the pickup row.

Bind off all stitches loosely in pattern.

Using the yarn needle, weave in all ends.

Ulst Mitered Scarf

DESIGNED BY LINDA CYR

No contemporary tweed book would be complete without at least one design featuring mitered squares and triangles. For this scarf, Linda uses two-color, garter-stitch stripes to make both squares and triangles. Nothing could be simpler. Rather than sewing the squares together once the scarf is complete, a triangle is joined to a square and then a square is joined along the other side of the just-knit triangle.

INTERMEDIATE

KNITTED MEASUREMENTS

Width 8" (20.5cm)

Length 64" (163cm)

MATERIALS

1 ball Tahki Yarns Donegal Tweed (100% pure new wool, 3½ oz [100g], 183 yd [167m]) each in #862 denim (A), #803 lime green (B), #863 crimson (C), #866 gray (D), and #839 khaki (E) (4) medium

Size 8 (5mm) needles, or size needed to obtain gauge

Size K-10½ (6.5mm) crochet hook

Yarn needle

Piece of cardboard about 5" (12.5cm) long (for tassels)

GAUGE

14 stitches and 28 rows = 4" (10cm) in garter stitch

TAKE TIME TO CHECK GAUGE.

ABBREVIATIONS AND TERMS

Dcd (double centered decrease) Slip 2 stitches together knitwise (as if to knit them together) to the right-hand needle, knit 1 stitch, pass both slipped stitches together over the knit stitch.

PATTERN STITCHES

Chain
Wrap the yarn around the crochet hook (yarn over), and draw it through the loop on the hook to form the first chain.

Garter Stitch
Knit every row.

Single Crochet
Insert the crochet hook in the stitch, yarn over and pull up a loop, yarn over and draw through both loops on the hook.

Slip Stitch
Insert the crochet hook in the stitch, yarn over and pull up a loop, and draw the loop through the loop on the hook.

Note: The scarf is worked in 8 mitered squares; the squares are joined with mitered triangles.

MITERED SQUARE

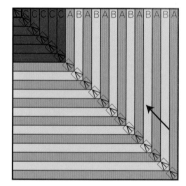

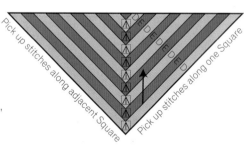

Pick up stitches along adjacent Square

Pick up stitches along one Square

 Yarn A

 Yarn B

 Yarn C

Yarn D

 Yarn E

 Dcd

SQUARES (MAKE 8)

Using A, cast on 43 stitches.

Row 1 K20, s2kp, k20.

Row 2 K20, p1, k20. Drop A (do not cut); join B.

Row 3 Using B, k19, s2kp, k19.

Row 4 K19, p1, k19. Drop B; pick up A.

Continue in garter stitch, alternating A and B every 2 rows and working dcd every other row, until 7 stripes of A have been completed. Cut A and B; join C.

Using C for the remainder of the Square, continue in garter stitch, working dcd every other row, until 3 stitches remain; work dcd—1 stitch remains.

Fasten off.

Referring to the layout diagram, arrange the Squares as shown.

Joining Triangles
Working with 2 adjacent Squares, join as follows:

Row 1 Using D, pick up and knit 21 stitches along the right-hand Square and 20 stitches along the left-hand Square (see diagram).

Row 2 K20, p1, k20. Drop D (do not cut); join E.

Row 3 Ssk, k17, s2kp, k17, k2tog.

Row 4 K18, p1, k18. Drop E; pick up D.

Continue in garter stitch, alternating D and E and working the shaping, until 3 stitches remain; work dcd—1 stitch remains. Fasten off.

Work a Joining Triangle on the opposite sides of these 2 Squares (see diagram); join the remaining Squares in the same way.

FINISHING

Block the pieces to the measurements, being careful not to flatten the texture.

Edging
Using the crochet hook and A, join the yarn with a slip stitch at one pointed end of the scarf.

Round 1 Chain 1, work 2 single crochet in the same stitch as joining, work single crochet evenly around the entire outer edge of the scarf, working 2 single crochet at the corners and 3 single crochet at the opposite point, work single crochet in the same stitch as the first single crochet, join with a slip stitch in the first single crochet.

Round 2 Chain 1, work 2 slip stitches in the same stitch as joining, work slip stitch evenly around the entire outer edge of the scarf, working additional slip stitches in the corners and at the opposite point, if necessary, to keep the edging flat, slip stitch in the same stitch as the beginning slip stitch, join with a slip stitch in the first stitch.

Fasten off.

Using the yarn needle, weave in all ends.

TASSELS

Using C, make two 5" (12.5cm) tassels; attach one to each point of the Scarf (see photo).

ASSEMBLY

Add Tassel

Pick up sts

Add Tassel

Dublin Cabled Vest

DESIGNED BY NORAH GAUGHAN

If you think of a sweater as landscape, this vest becomes a rugged, windswept countryside full of rolling hills, rocks, and dried branches in the British Isles.

A good tip for working from a cable chart is to make a copy of the chart and follow along it row by row. I always use sticky notes (several to cover the width of the chart) and move them along as I knit. After a while, the adhesive of the notes will disappear and you will need to replace them with a fresh supply.

INTERMEDIATE

SIZES

Small (Medium, Large, 1X, 2X)

KNITTED MEASUREMENTS

Chest 37½ (42, 45½, 49, 52½)" (95 [106.5, 115.5, 124.5, 133.5]cm)

Length 24 (24, 25, 26, 26)" (61 [61, 63.5, 66, 66]cm)

MATERIALS

5 (5, 6, 6, 6) skeins Tahki Yarns Donegal Tweed (100% pure new wool, 3½ oz [100g], 183 yd [167m]) in #867 taupe (4) worsted

Size 7 (4.5mm) and size 8 (5mm) needles, or size needed to obtain gauge

Size 7 (4.5mm) circular needle, 30" (76cm) long

Cable needle

Stitch markers

Yarn needle

6 leather buttons, 1" (25mm) in diameter

GAUGE

22 stitches and 24 rows = 4" (10cm) in cable pattern, using the larger needles

TAKE TIME TO CHECK GAUGE.

PATTERN STITCHES

Fancy Rib
(multiple of 10 stitches + 1 extra stitch)
Row 1 (wrong side) P1, k1, p2, k3, p2, *[k1, p1] twice, p1, k3, p2; repeat from * across to the last 2 stitches, end k1, p1.
Row 2 Knit the knit stitches and purl the purl stitches as they face you. Repeat row 2 for fancy rib.

Cable Pattern
See chart.

Notes: The cable pattern begins with a wrong-side row; begin working the chart from left to right for row 1.

Most sizes show partial cables at the beginning and end of rows. DO NOT work partial cables; continue working stitches in rib as row 1 of the chart or work in background stitches, as desired.

When working the armhole and neck shaping, do not work partial cables; work those stitches in rib.

CABLE CHART

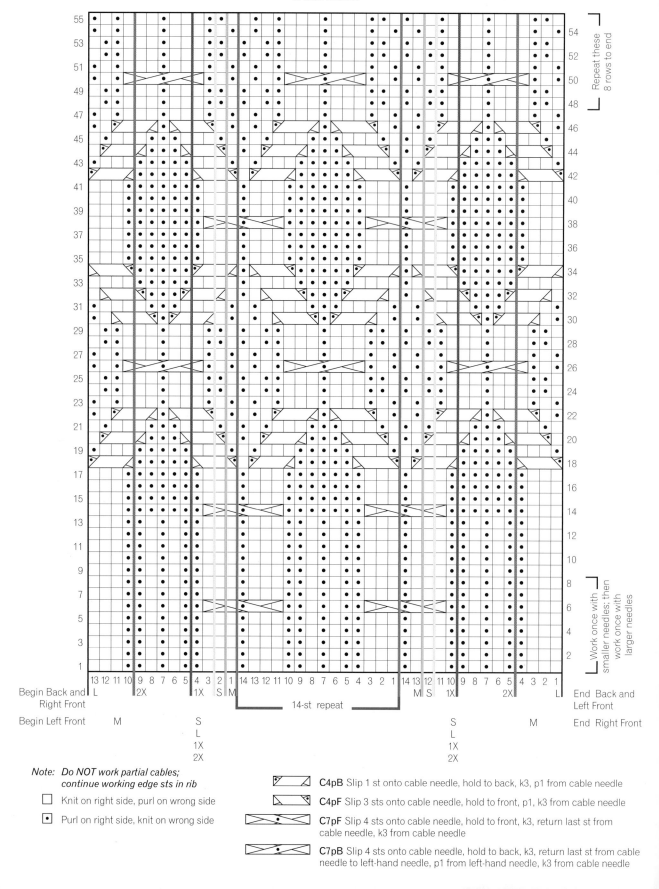

Note: *Do NOT work partial cables;*
continue working edge sts in rib

☐ Knit on right side, purl on wrong side

▪ Purl on right side, knit on wrong side

C4pB Slip 1 st onto cable needle, hold to back, k3, p1 from cable needle

C4pF Slip 3 sts onto cable needle, hold to front, p1, k3 from cable needle

C7pF Slip 4 sts onto cable needle, hold to front, k3, return last st from cable needle, k3 from cable needle

C7pB Slip 4 sts onto cable needle, hold to back, k3, return last st from cable needle to left-hand needle, p1 from left-hand needle, k3 from cable needle

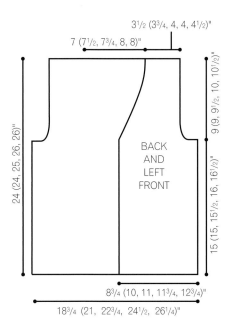

7 ($7^{1/2}$, $7^{3/4}$, 8, 8)"

$3^{1/2}$ ($3^{3/4}$, 4, 4, $4^{1/2}$)"

9 (9, $9^{1/2}$, 10, $10^{1/2}$)"

BACK
AND
LEFT
FRONT

24 (24, 25, 26, 26)"

15 (15, $15^{1/2}$, 16, $16^{1/2}$)"

$8^{3/4}$ (10, 11, $11^{3/4}$, $12^{3/4}$)"

$18^{3/4}$ (21, $22^{3/4}$, $24^{1/2}$, $26^{1/4}$)"

BACK

Using the smaller needles, cast on 103 (115, 125, 135, 145) stitches.

Begin Pattern from Chart

(Wrong side) Begin at the left-hand side of the chart as indicated for desired size—with stitch 2 (1, 13, 4, 9); work 14-stitch repeat 7 (8, 7, 9, 9) times, end with stitch 12 (13, 1, 10, 5) at the right-hand side of the chart; work even for 8 rows total, ending with a right-side row.

(Wrong side) Change to the larger needles; repeat rows 1–8 of the chart once—16 rows worked.

(Wrong side) Work rows 9–55 once, then repeat rows 48–55 for the remainder of the garment.

Continue working from the chart until the piece measures 15 (15, $15^{1/2}$, 16, $16^{1/2}$)" (38 [38, 39.5, 40.5, 42]cm) from the beginning, ending with a wrong-side row.

Shape Armhole

(Right side) Bind off 5 (6, 6, 7, 7) stitches at the beginning of the next 2 rows, then 3 (4, 4, 5, 6) stitches at the beginning of the next 2 rows, then 2 (3, 4, 5, 6) stitches at the beginning of the next 2 rows—83 (89, 97, 101, 107) stitches remain.

(Right side) Decrease 1 stitch each side every other row 3 (3, 4, 5, 6) times—77 (83, 89, 91, 95) stitches remain. Work even until the armhole measures 9 (9, $9^{1/2}$, 10, $10^{1/2}$)" (23 [23, 24, 25.5, 26.5]cm) from the beginning of the shaping, ending with a wrong-side row.

Shape Shoulders and Neck

(Right side) Bind off 19 (21, 23, 23, 25) stitches at the beginning of the next 2 rows for the shoulders—39 (41, 43, 45, 45) stitches remain for the neck.

Bind off the remaining stitches.

LEFT FRONT

Using the smaller needles, cast on 49 (55, 60, 65, 70) stitches.

Begin Pattern from Chart

(Wrong side) Begin at the left-hand side of the chart—with stitch 4 (11, 4, 4, 4); work 14-stitch repeat 3 (3, 3, 4, 4) times, end with stitch 12 (13, 1, 10, 5) at the right-hand side of the chart; work even for 8 rows total, ending with a right-side row.

(Wrong side) Change to the larger needles; repeat rows 1–8 of the chart once—16 rows worked.

(Wrong side) Work rows 9–55 once, then repeat rows 48–55 for the remainder of the garment.

Continue working from the chart until the piece measures 15 (15, $15^{1/2}$, 16, $16^{1/2}$)" (38 [38, 39.5, 40.5, 42]cm) from the beginning, ending with a wrong-side row.

Shape Armhole and Neck

(Right side) At the armhole edge, bind off 5 (6, 6, 7, 7) stitches once, then 3 (4, 4, 5, 6) stitches once, then 2 (3, 4, 5, 6) stitches once.

(Right side) At the armhole edge, decrease 1 stitch every other row 3 (3, 4, 5, 6) times; AT THE SAME TIME, beginning the first row of the neck shaping, work across to the last 3 stitches, k2tog, p1.

(Right side) At the neck edge (the end of the right-side rows), decrease 1 stitch every other row 8 (10, 12, 12, 13) times, then every 4 rows 8 (7, 6, 7, 6) times, working the armhole edge even while completing the neck shaping—19 (21, 23, 23, 25) stitches remain for the shoulder.

Work even until the armhole measures 9 (9, 9½, 10, 10½)" (23 [23, 24, 25.5, 26.5]cm) from the beginning of the shaping, ending with a wrong-side row.

Bind off the remaining stitches.

RIGHT FRONT

Using the smaller needles, cast on 49 (55, 60, 65, 70) stitches.

Begin Pattern from Chart
(Wrong side) Begin at the left-hand side of the chart—with stitch 2 (1, 13, 4, 9); work 14-stitch repeat 3 (3, 3, 4, 4) times, end with stitch 10 (3, 10, 10, 10) of the next repeat at the right-hand side of the chart; work even for 8 rows total, ending with a right-side row.

(Wrong side) Change to the larger needles; repeat rows 1–8 of the chart once—16 rows worked.

(Wrong side) Work rows 9–55 once, then repeat rows 48–55 for the remainder of the garment.

Continue working from the chart until the piece measures 15 (15, 15½, 16, 16½)" (38 [38, 39.5, 40.5, 42]cm) from the beginning, ending with a right-side row.

Shape Armhole and Neck
(Wrong side) At the armhole edge, bind off 5 (6, 6, 7, 7) stitches once, then 3 (4, 4, 5, 6) stitches once, then 2 (3, 4, 5, 6) stitches once.

(Wrong side) At the armhole edge, decrease 1 stitch every other row 3 (3, 4, 5, 6) times; AT THE SAME TIME, beginning the first row of neck shaping, work across to the last 3 stitches, p2tog, k1.

(Right side) At the neck edge (the beginning of the right-side rows), decrease 1 stitch (p1, k2tog) every other row 8 (10, 12, 12, 13) times, then every 4 rows 8 (7, 6, 7, 6) times, working the armhole edge even while completing the neck shaping—19 (21, 23, 23, 25) stitches remain for the shoulder.

Work even until the armhole measures 9 (9, 9½, 10, 10½)" (23 [23, 24, 25.5, 26.5]cm) from the beginning of the shaping, ending with a wrong-side row.

Bind off the remaining stitches.

FINISHING

Block the pieces to the measurements, being careful not to flatten the texture. Sew the shoulder seams.

Right Front Neck and Button Band
With the right side facing, using the circular needle and beginning at the lower Front edge, pick up and knit 151 (153, 157, 161, 165) stitches up the right Front, along the neck shaping and across to the center Back neck.

Begin Pattern
(Wrong side) K0 (0, 3, 0, 1), p0 (0, 2, 0, 2), k0 (2, 1, 0, 1); work fancy rib across 151 (151, 151, 161, 161) stitches. Continue in this way, knitting the knit stitches and purling the purl stitches as they face you, until the band measures 1½" (3.8cm) from the pickup row.

Bind off all stitches loosely in rib.

Left Front Neck and Buttonhole Band
Place markers for 6 buttonholes on the left Front, with the first one ½" (13mm) from the lower edge, the last one ½" (13mm) below the beginning of the neck shaping, and the remaining 4 evenly spaced between.

Begin Pattern
(Wrong side) Work fancy rib across 151 (151, 151, 161, 161) stitches, end k0 (0, 1, 0, 1), p0 (0, 2, 0, 2), k0 (2, 3, 0, 1).

Work as for the right Front band for 3 rows.

Buttonhole Row Work in pattern to the first marker, *[work 2 stitches together in pattern, yarn over] for the buttonhole, work to the next marker; repeat from * for the remaining buttonholes, work to end.

Complete as for the button band. Sew the seam at the Back neck.

Armhole Bands
With the right side facing, using the smaller needles and beginning at the underarm, pick up and knit 111 (111, 115, 119, 121) stitches around the armhole.

Begin Pattern

(Wrong side) [K1, p1] 0 (0, 1, 2, 0) time(s), work 111 (111, 111, 111, 121) stitches in fancy rib, end [k1, p1] 0 (0, 1, 2, 0) time(s). Work even until the band measures 1½" (3.8cm) from the pickup row.

Bind off all stitches in pattern.

Sew the side seams.

Using the yarn needle, weave in all ends. Sew on the buttons opposite the buttonholes.

Harris-Style Sampler Cardigan

DESIGNED BY NANCY J. THOMAS

The easy wide stripes and changing texture patterns make this stitch sampler fun to knit. All stitches consist of uncomplicated knit and purl stitches. Are you a purple/fuchsia/teal person, or do you love rich autumn shades? Our tweed, fringed cardigan offers you both options. Choosing colors for a sweater can be challenging; looking at small pieces or skeins of yarn leaves a lot to the imagination. If you want other colors, choose three bolder shades tempered with several subtler colors. Think about the order of the colors. What color do you want next to your face?

INTERMEDIATE

SIZES
Small (Medium, Large, 1X, 2X)

KNITTED MEASUREMENTS
Bust 34 (38, 42, 46, 50)" (86 [96.5, 106.5, 117, 127]cm)

Length 20½ (21, 21½, 22, 22½)" (52 [53.5, 54.5, 56, 57]cm)

MATERIALS
Olive Version 2 (3, 3, 3, 4) skeins Tahki Yarns Donegal Tweed (100% pure new wool, 3½ oz [100g], 183 yd [167m]) in #803 olive (A), 1 (1, 1, 2, 2) skein(s) in #845 eggplant (B), 2 (2, 2, 2, 3) skeins in #874 deep red (C), 1 (1, 1, 1, 2) skein(s) in #893 pumpkin (D), and 1 (1, 2, 2, 2) skein(s) in #895 charcoal (E)
🍥 medium

Teal Version (page 105) 2 (3, 3, 3, 4) skeins Tahki Yarns Donegal Tweed (100% pure new wool, 3½ oz [100g], 183 yd [167m]) in #809 teal (A), 1 (1, 1, 2, 2) skein(s) in #849 plum (B), 2 (2, 2, 2, 3) skeins in #896 purple (C), 1 (1, 1, 1, 2) skein(s) in #866 medium gray (D), and 1 (1, 2, 2, 2) skein(s) in #810 fuchsia (E)

Both Versions Size 7 (4.5mm) and size 8 (5mm) needles, or size needed to obtain gauge

Stitch markers

Stitch holders

Yarn needle

Size G-6 (4.5mm) crochet hook (for Fringe)

4 buttons 1" (25mm)

GAUGE
18 stitches and 24 rows = 4" (10cm) in stockinette stitch, using the larger needles

TAKE TIME TO CHECK GAUGE.

SPECIAL TECHNIQUE
Edge Stitches At the left Front edge, slip the first stitch of every wrong-side row knitwise, purl the last stitch of every right-side row; at the right Front, slip the first stitch of every right-side row knitwise, purl the last stitch of every wrong-side row.

PATTERN STITCHES
(see charts)

Stockinette Stitch
Knit on the right side, purl on the wrong side.

K2, P2 Rib (multiple of 4 stitches + 2 extra stitches)
Row 1 (right side) K2, *p2, k2; repeat from * across.
Row 2 Knit the knit stitches and purl the purl stitches as they face you. Repeat row 2 for k2, p2 rib.

Seed Stitch (multiple of 2 stitches + 1 extra stitch)
Row 1 (right side) *K1, p1; repeat from * across.
Row 2 (wrong side) Purl the knit stitches and knit the purl stitches as they face you.
Repeat row 2 for seed stitch.

SEED STITCH
2 stitch/2 row repeat

☐ Knit on right side, purl on wrong side

▣ Purl on right side, knit on wrong side

Double Seed Stitch (multiple of 2 stitches)
Row 1 (right side) *P1, k1; repeat from * across.
Row 2 Knit the knit stitches and purl the purl stitches as they face you.
Row 3 *K1, p1; repeat from * across.
Row 4 Knit the knit stitches and purl the purl stitches as they face you.
Repeat rows 1–4 for double seed stitch.

DOUBLE SEED STITCH
2 stitch/4 row repeat

☐ Knit on right side, purl on wrong side

▣ Purl on right side, knit on wrong side

Garter Basket Weave
(multiple of 6 stitches + 3 extra stitches)
Rows 1, 3, and 5 (right side) *P3, k3; repeat from * across to the last 3 stitches, p3.
Rows 2, 4, 6, and 8 Purl.
Rows 7 and 9 Knit.
Rows 10, 12, and 14 *P3, k3; repeat from * across to the last 3 stitches, p3.
Rows 11, 13, 15, and 17 Knit.
Rows 16 and 18 Purl.
Repeat rows 1–18 for garter basket weave.

GARTER BASKET WEAVE

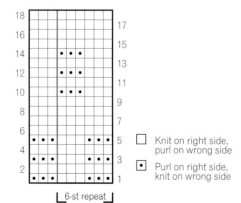

☐ Knit on right side, purl on wrong side

▣ Purl on right side, knit on wrong side

K3, P3 Basket Weave
(multiple of 6 stitches + 3 extra stitches)
Rows 1 and 3 (right side) *P3, k3; repeat from * across to the last 3 stitches, p3.
Row 2 and all wrong-side rows Knit the knit stitches and purl the purl stitches as they face you.
Rows 5 and 7 *K3, p3; repeat from * across to the last 3 stitches, k3.
Row 8 Repeat row 2.
Repeat rows 1–8 for k3, p3 basket weave.

K3, P3 BASKET WEAVE
6 stitch/8 row repeat

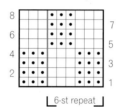

☐ Knit on right side, purl on wrong side

▣ Purl on right side, knit on wrong side

K2, P2 Basket Weave
(multiple of 4 stitches + 2 extra stitches)
Row 1 (right side) *K2, p2; repeat from * across to the last 2 stitches, k2.
Row 2 Purl.
Repeat rows 1 and 2 for k2, p2 basket weave.

K2, P2 BASKET WEAVE

☐ Knit on right side, purl on wrong side

▣ Purl on right side, knit on wrong side

Stripe Sequence
In seed stitch, using A, work 5½" (14cm), ending with a wrong-side row, fasten off A, join B; in double seed stitch, using B, work 2½" (6.5cm), ending with a wrong-side row; in garter basket weave, using C, work 5" (12.5cm), end as indicated in instructions, then begin armhole shaping; in k3, p3 basket weave, using D, work 12 rows; in k2, p2 basket weave, using E, work for remainder of the piece.

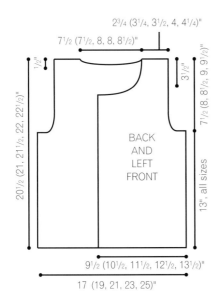

BACK

Using the larger needles and A, cast on 77 (85, 95, 103, 113) stitches.

(Right side) Begin the stripe sequence, working the patterns and colors indicated; work even until the piece measures 8" (20.5cm) from the beginning, increase 1 (0, 1, 0, 1) stitch(es), decrease 0 (1, 0, 1, 0) stitch(es) across the last (wrong-side) row in double seed stitch using B—78 (84, 96, 102, 114) stitches.

Fasten off B; join C.

Begin Garter Basket Weave
(Right side) Beginning row 1, work 6-stitch multiple of garter basket weave across.

Work even until the piece measures 13" (33cm) from the beginning, ending (wrong-side) row 14 or 16 of the pattern; make a note of the last row worked.

Fasten off C; join D.

Shape Armhole
(Right side) Continuing in the stripe sequence, using D, bind off 3 (3, 4, 4, 6) stitches at the beginning of the next 2 rows, then 2 (2, 3, 4, 4) stitches at the beginning of the next 2 rows—68 (74, 82, 86, 94) stitches remain.

(Right side) Decrease 1 stitch each side every other row 4 (5, 7, 7, 9) times; AT THE SAME TIME, when 12 rows of D have been worked, change to E as

indicated in the stripe sequence—60 (64, 68, 72, 76) stitches remain. Work even until the armhole measures 7 (7½, 8, 8½, 9)" (18 [19, 20.5, 21.5, 23]cm) from the beginning of the shaping, ending with a wrong-side row; place a marker each side of center 26 (26, 28, 28, 30) stitches.

Shape Neck and Shoulders
(Right side) Work across to the first marker; join a second ball of yarn and bind off the center stitches, work to end—17 (19, 20, 22, 23) stitches remain each side. Working both sides at the same time, at each neck edge bind off 2 stitches twice—13 (15, 16, 18, 19) stitches remain on each side for the shoulder.

Bind off the remaining stitches.

LEFT FRONT

Using the larger needles and A, cast on 43 (47, 53, 57, 61) stitches.

(Right side) Begin the stripe sequence, working the patterns and colors indicated; work even until the piece measures 8" (20.5cm) from the beginning, decrease 0 (1, 1, 2, 0) stitch(es) across the last (wrong-side) row in double seed stitch using B—43 (46, 52, 55, 61) stitches remain.

Fasten off B; join C.

Begin Garter Basket Weave

(Right side) Beginning row 1, work 6-stitch multiple of garter basket weave across, beginning p3, end k3 (p3, p3, k3, k3), p1 (edge stitch).

Work even until the piece measures 13" (33cm) from the beginning, end same wrong-side row as for the Back.

Fasten off C; join D.

Shape Armhole

(Right side) Continuing in the stripe sequence using D, at the armhole edge bind off 3 (3, 4, 4, 6) stitches once, then 2 (2, 3, 4, 4) stitches once—38 (41, 45, 47, 51) stitches remain.

(Right side) At the armhole edge, decrease 1 stitch every other row 4 (5, 7, 7, 9) times; AT THE SAME TIME, when 12 rows of D have been worked, change to E as indicated in the stripe sequence—34 (36, 38, 40, 42) stitches remain. Work even until the armhole measures 4 (4½, 5, 5½, 6)" (10 [11.5, 12.5, 14, 15]cm) from the beginning of the shaping, ending with a wrong-side row.

Shape Neck

(Right side) Work across to the last 13 (13, 14, 14, 15) stitches; place stitches on a holder for the neck, turn.

(Wrong side) Beginning this row, decrease 1 stitch at the neck edge (beginning of the wrong-side rows, end of the right-side rows) every row 5 times, then every other row 3 times—13 (15, 16, 18, 19) stitches remain for the shoulder.

Work even until the armhole measures 7½ (8, 8½, 9, 9½)" (19 [20.5, 21.5, 23, 24]cm) from the beginning of the shaping, ending with a wrong-side row.

(Right side) Bind off the remaining stitches.

Place markers for 4 buttons on the left Front edge, with the first one 2½" (6.5cm) from the lower edge, the last one at the neck edge (this buttonhole will be worked as part of the neck band), and the remaining 2 evenly spaced between (see the photo for suggested spacing).

RIGHT FRONT

Using the larger needles and A, cast on 43 (47, 53, 57, 61) stitches.

(Right side) Begin the stripe sequence, working the patterns and colors indicated, and AT THE SAME TIME, work the buttonholes opposite the first 3 markers as follows:

(Right side) Buttonhole Row At the center Front edge, work 3 stitches in pattern, bind off 2 stitches for the buttonhole, work to end.

(Wrong side) Work across to the bound-off stitches, cast on 2 stitches, work to end.

Work even until the piece measures 8" (20.5cm) from the beginning, decrease 0 (1, 1, 2, 0) stitch(es) across the last (wrong-side) row in double seed stitch using B—43 (46, 52, 55, 61) stitches remain. Fasten off B; join C.

Begin Garter Basket Weave

(Right side) P1 (edge stitch), beginning row 1, work 6-stitch multiple of garter basket weave across, beginning p3 (k3, k3, p3, p3), ending k3.

Work even until the piece measures 13" (33cm) from the beginning, ending same wrong-side row as for the Back. Fasten off C; join D. Continuing in the stripe sequence, using D, work 1 row even.

Shape Armhole

(Wrong side) At the armhole edge, bind off 3 (3, 4, 4, 6) stitches once, then 2 (2, 3, 4, 4) stitches once—38 (41, 45, 47, 51) stitches remain.

(Wrong side) At the armhole edge, decrease 1 stitch every other row 4 (5, 7, 7, 9) times; AT THE SAME TIME, when 12 rows of D have been worked, change to E as indicated in the stripe sequence—34 (36, 38, 40, 42) stitches remain. Work even until the armhole measures 4 (4½, 5, 5½, 6)" (10 [11.5, 12.5, 14, 15]cm) from the beginning of the shaping, ending with a wrong-side row.

Shape Neck

(Right side) Work across the first 13 (13, 14, 14, 15) stitches, place the stitches on a holder for the neck, work to end.

(Wrong side) Beginning this row, decrease 1 stitch at the neck edge (end of the wrong-side rows, beginning of the right-side rows) every row 5 times, then every other row 3 times—13 (15, 16, 18, 19) stitches remain for the shoulder.

Work even until the armhole measures 7½ (8, 8½, 9, 9½)" (19 [20.5, 21.5, 23, 24]cm) from the beginning of the shaping, ending with a right-side row.

(Wrong side) Bind off the remaining stitches.

SLEEVES (MAKE 2)

Using the smaller needles and A, cast on 42 (46, 46, 50, 50) stitches.

(Right side) Begin k2, p2 rib; work even until the piece measures 4 (4½, 4½, 5, 5)" (10 [11.5, 11.5, 12.5, 12.5]cm) from the beginning, increasing 3 stitches evenly across the last (wrong-side) row—45 (49, 49, 53, 53) stitches.

(Right side) Continuing with A, change to the larger needles and the stripe sequence. Work even for 10 (10, 8, 8, 6) rows, ending with a wrong-side row.

Shape Sleeve
(Right side) Beginning this row, increase 1 stitch each side every 10 (10, 8, 8, 6) rows 7 (7, 9, 9, 12) times; AT THE SAME TIME, change to B when the piece measures 9½ (10, 10, 10½, 10½)" (24 [25.5, 25.5, 26.5, 26.5]cm) from the beginning (5½" [14cm] above the ribbing), as given in the stripe sequence. When the piece measures 12 (12½, 12½, 13, 13)" (30.5 [32, 32, 33, 33]cm) from the beginning, change to C and garter basket weave, centering the pattern on the sleeve—59 (63, 67, 71, 77) stitches when shaping is completed.

Work even until the piece measures 17 (17½, 17½, 18, 18)" (43 [44.5, 44.5, 45.5, 45.5]cm) from the beginning, ending with the same wrong-side row of the pattern as for the Back armhole.

Shape Cap
(Right side) Continuing in the stripe sequence, using D, bind off 3 (3, 4, 4, 6) stitches at the beginning of the next 2 rows, then 2 (2, 3, 4, 4) stitches at the beginning of the next 2 rows—49 (53, 53, 55, 57) stitches remain.

(Right side) Decrease 1 stitch each side every other row 13 times, changing to E after 12 rows of D, as indicated in the stripe sequence—23 (27, 27, 29, 31) stitches remain.

Bind off 3 (4, 4, 4, 5) stitches at the beginning of the next 4 rows—11 (11, 11, 13, 11) stitches remain.

Bind off the remaining stitches.

FINISHING

Block the pieces to the measurements. Sew the shoulder seams. Set in the Sleeves, matching the pattern; sew the side and sleeve seams.

Neck Band
With the right side facing, using the smaller needles and E, beginning at the right Front neck, place 13 (13, 14, 14, 15) stitches from the holder onto the needle; slip 1 (edge stitch), k2, bind off 2 for the buttonhole, knit the remaining stitches from the holder; pick up and knit 26 along the neck shaping to the Back neck, 26 (26, 28, 28, 30) stitches across the Back neck, 26 stitches along the neck shaping to the left Front holder; k13 (13, 14, 14, 15) stitches from the holder—104 (104, 108, 108, 112) stitches.

Begin Pattern
(Wrong side) Slip 1 (edge stitch), beginning p2, work in k2, p2 rib across to the last stitch, p1 (edge stitch).

Work even for 5 rows, ending with a right-side row.

(Wrong side) Bind off all stitches loosely in rib.

Using the yarn needle, weave in all ends. Sew on the buttons opposite the buttonholes.

FRINGE

From A, C, and E, cut strands 5" (12.5cm) long. Using 1 strand of each color held together, attach the Fringe to the right Front, spaced approximately ½" (13mm) apart.

Chapter 7

SAILING THE NORTH SEA

Projects for Advanced Knitters

The designs in this chapter will certainly offer you a challenge, but by no means do you need to be an expert knitter—just one who loves projects with multiple details. Some details involve stitch patterns, and others such skills as working with multiple colors. Push the envelope by trying a new, untried technique, or simplify the design if you feel it's too much for you. Your simplification can be as small as substituting a pattern that you find less challenging.

The highlights of this chapter are the two throws, the Outer Hebrides Sampler Throw (page 124) and the Lake District Throw (page 134), which offer flowers and leaves in patterns that involve both color and stitch patterning. The stitch throw consists of simple blocks of color, and the floral throw is a combination of intarsia, stranding, and duplicate stitch. Both are sure to be conversation pieces.

Isle of Skye Jacket

DESIGNED BY POONAM THAKUR

This cabled jacket is covered with beautiful ropey cables. Notice that four types of cables are given in the cable A pattern. Each set of cables are worked as either all knit stitches or a combination of knit and purl stitches. Look at the cables in the charts for a visual representation of what happens as you knit.

INTERMEDIATE

SIZES

Small (Medium, Large, 1X, 2X)

KNITTED MEASUREMENTS

Bust 36 (40, 44, 48, 52)" (91 [101.5, 112, 122, 132]cm)

Length 22 (23, 23½, 24, 24½)" (56 [58.5, 59.5, 61, 62]cm)

Note: Because cabled fabric is stretchy, the garment may be blocked to larger sizes, if desired.

MATERIALS

5 (5, 6, 7, 8) skeins Tahki Yarns Donegal Tweed (100% pure new wool, 3½ oz [100g], 183 yd [167m]) in #863 red (4) medium

Size 7 (4.5mm) and size 9 (5.5mm) needles, or size needed to obtain gauge

Size 7 (4.5mm) circular needle, 16" (40cm) long (for collar) (optional)

Cable needle

Stitch holders

Stitch markers

Yarn needle

7 buttons, 1" (25mm) in diameter

GAUGE

18 stitches and 26 rows = 4" (10cm) in reverse stockinette stitch, using the larger needles; cable B measures approximately 1" (2.5cm) and cable A measures approximately 3¼" (8.5cm) at the widest point

TAKE TIME TO CHECK GAUGE.

ABBREVIATIONS AND TERMS

C4B Slip 2 stitches onto a cable needle and hold to the back, knit 2 stitches, knit 2 stitches from the cable needle.

C4F Slip 2 stitches onto a cable needle and hold to the front, knit 2 stitches, knit 2 stitches from the cable needle.

C5pB Slip 2 stitches onto a cable needle and hold to the back, knit 3 stitches, purl 2 stitches from the cable needle.

C5pF Slip 3 stitches onto a cable needle and hold to the front, purl 2 stitches, knit 3 stitches from the cable needle.

C6B Slip 3 stitches onto a cable needle and hold to the back, knit 3 stitches, knit 3 stitches from the cable needle.

C6F Slip 3 stitches onto a cable needle and hold to the front, knit 3 stitches, knit 3 stitches from the cable needle.

Tw4pB Slip 1 stitch onto a cable needle and hold to the back, knit 3 stitches, purl 1 stitch from the cable needle.

Tw4pF Slip 3 stitches onto a cable needle and hold to the front, purl 1 stitch, knit 3 stitches from the cable needle.

PATTERN STITCHES

K2, P2 Rib (multiple of 4 stitches + 2 extra stitches)
Row 1 (right side) *K2, p2; repeat from *, end k2.
Row 2 *P2, k2; repeat from *, end p2.
Repeat rows 1 and 2 for k2, p2 rib.

Reverse Stockinette Stitch

Purl on the right side, knit on the wrong side.

CABLE A

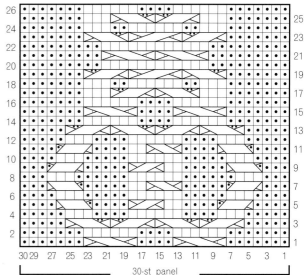

30-st panel

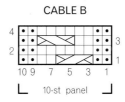

CABLE B

10-st panel

Knit on right side, purl on wrong side			
Purl on right side, knit on wrong side			
	C4B		
	C4F		
	Tw4pB		
	Tw4pF		
	C5pB		
	C5pF		
	C6B		
	C6F		

Cable Pattern A (panel of 30 stitches; see chart)
Row 1 (right side) P7, C6F, p4, C6F, p7.
Row 2 and all wrong-side rows Knit the knit stitches and purl the purl stitches as they face you.
Row 3 P5, [C5pB, C5pF] twice, p5.
Row 5 P4, Tw4pB, p4, k2, C4B, p4, Tw4pF, p4.
Row 7 P3, Tw4pB, p5, C4F, k2, p5, Tw4pF, p3.
Row 9 P3, Tw4pF, p5, k2, C4B, p5, Tw4pB, p3.
Row 11 P4, Tw4pF, p4, C4F, k2, p4, Tw4pB, p4.
Row 13 P5, [C5pF, C5pB] twice, p5.
Row 15 P7, C6F, p4, C6F, p7.
Row 17 P7, k3, C5pF, C5pB, k3, p7.
Row 19 P7, C5pF, C6B, C5pB, p7.
Row 21 P9, [C6F] twice, p9.
Row 23 P7, C5pB, C6B, C5pF, p7.
Row 25 P7, k3, C5pB, C5pF, k3, p7.
Row 26 Repeat row 2.
Repeat rows 1–26 for cable A.

Cable B (panel of 10 stitches; see chart)
Row 1 (right side) P2, C4B, k2, p2.
Row 2 K2, p6, k2.
Row 3 P2, k2, C4F, p2.
Row 4 K2, p6, k2.
Repeat rows 1–4 for cable B.

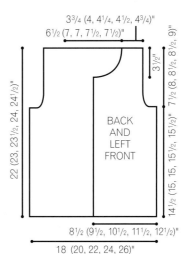

3³/₄ (4, 4¹/₄, 4¹/₂, 4³/₄)"
6¹/₂ (7, 7, 7¹/₂, 7¹/₂)"
3¹/₂"
7¹/₂ (8, 8¹/₂, 8¹/₂, 9)"
22 (23, 23¹/₂, 24, 24¹/₂)"
14¹/₂ (15, 15, 15¹/₂, 15¹/₂)"
BACK AND LEFT FRONT
8¹/₂ (9¹/₂, 10¹/₂, 11¹/₂, 12¹/₂)"
18 (20, 22, 24, 26)"

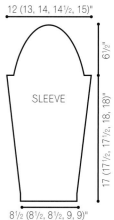

12 (13, 14, 14¹/₂, 15)"
6¹/₂"
SLEEVE
17 (17¹/₂, 17¹/₂, 18, 18)"
8¹/₂ (8¹/₂, 8¹/₂, 9, 9)"

BACK

Using the smaller needles, cast on 106 (114, 122, 130, 138) stitches.

(Right side) Begin k2, p2 rib, end k2; work even until the piece measures 2" (5cm) from the beginning, increase 8 stitches evenly spaced across the last (wrong-side) row—114 (122, 130, 138, 146) stitches.

Change to the larger needles.

Begin Pattern
(Right side) P2 (4, 6, 8, 10), work cable B across 10 stitches, *p0 (1, 2, 3, 4), work cable A across 30 stitches, p0 (1, 2, 3, 4)*, [work cable B across 10 stitches] 3 times; repeat * to * once, work cable B across 10 stitches, p2 (4, 6, 8, 10).

Work even in pattern, working stitches at each side and between cable patterns in reverse stockinette stitch, until the piece measures 14½ (15, 15, 15½, 15½)" (37 [38, 38, 39.5, 39.5]cm) from the beginning, ending with a wrong-side row.

Shape Armhole
(Right side) Bind off 2 (3, 4, 5, 6) stitches at the beginning of the next 4 rows—106 (110, 114, 118, 122) stitches remain.

(Right side) Decrease 1 stitch on each side every other row 8 times—90 (94, 98, 102, 106) stitches remain. Work even until the armhole measures 7½ (8, 8½, 8½, 9)" (19 [20.5, 21.5, 21.5, 23]cm) from the beginning of the shaping, ending with a wrong-side row.

Shape Shoulders and Neck
(Right side) Bind off 24 (25, 27, 28, 30) stitches at the beginning of the next 2 rows—42 (44, 44, 46, 46) stitches remain for the neck.

Place the remaining stitches on a holder.

LEFT FRONT

Using the smaller needles, cast on 50 (54, 58, 62, 66) stitches.

(Right side) Begin k2, p2 rib, end k2; work even until the piece measures 2" (5cm) from the beginning, increase 4 stitches evenly spaced across the last (wrong-side) row—54 (58, 62, 66, 70) stitches.

Change to the larger needles.

Begin Pattern
(Right side) P2 (4, 6, 8, 10), work cable B across 10 stitches, p0 (1, 2, 3, 4), work cable A across 30 stitches, p0 (1, 2, 3, 4), work cable B across 10 stitches, p2.

Work even in pattern, working stitches at each side and between cable patterns in reverse stockinette stitch, until the piece measures 14½ (15, 15, 15½, 15½)" (37 [38, 38, 39.5, 39.5]cm) from the beginning, ending with a wrong-side row.

Shape Armhole
(Right side) At the armhole edge, bind off 2 (3, 4, 5, 6) stitches once, then 2 (3, 4, 5, 6) stitches once—50 (52, 54, 56, 58) stitches remain.

(Right side) At the armhole edge, decrease 1 stitch every other row 8 times—42 (44, 46, 48, 50) stitches remain. Work even until the armhole measures 4 (4½, 5, 5, 5½)" (10 [11.5, 12.5, 12.5, 14]cm) from the beginning of the shaping, ending with a wrong-side row.

Shape Neck
(Right side) Work across to the last 8 (9, 9, 10, 10) stitches, place the remaining stitches on the holder, turn—34 (35, 37, 38, 40) stitches remain.

(Wrong side) At the neck edge (beginning of the wrong-side rows, end of the right-side rows), decrease 1 stitch every row 4 times, then every other row 6 times—24 (25, 27, 28, 30) stitches remain for the shoulder.

Work even until the armhole measures the same as for the Back to the shoulder; bind off the remaining stitches.

RIGHT FRONT

Work as for the Left Front for ribbing.

Change to the larger needles.

Begin Pattern
(Right side) P2, work cable B across 10 stitches, p0 (1, 2, 3, 4), work cable A across 30 stitches, p0 (1, 2, 3, 4), work cable B across 10 stitches, p2 (4, 6, 8, 10).

Continue as for the Left Front, reversing all shaping by working the armhole and shoulder bind-off at the beginning of the wrong-side rows and the neck shaping at the beginning of the right-side rows.

SLEEVES (MAKE 2)

Using the smaller needles, cast on 46 (46, 50, 50, 50) stitches.

(Right side) Begin k2, p2 rib, end k2; work even until the piece measures 2" (5cm) from the beginning, increase 4 (6, 4, 6, 8) stitches evenly spaced across the last (wrong-side) row—50 (52, 54 56, 58) stitches.

Change to the larger needles.

Begin Pattern
(Right side) P0 (1, 2, 3, 4), work cable B across 10 stitches, cable A across 30 stitches, cable B across 10 stitches, p0 (1, 2, 3, 4).

Work even in pattern, working stitches at each side and between cable patterns in reverse stockinette stitch, for 5 rows, ending with a wrong-side row.

Shape Sleeve
(Right side) Continuing in pattern, beginning this row, increase 1 stitch each side every 10 (8, 8, 6, 6) rows 8 (10, 11, 12, 13) times, working increased stitches in reverse stockinette stitch—66 (72, 76, 80, 84) stitches.

Work even until the piece measures 17 (17½, 17½, 18, 18)" (43 [44.5, 44.5, 45.5, 45.5]cm) from the beginning, ending with a wrong-side row.

Shape Cap
(Right side) Bind off 2 (3, 4, 5, 6) stitches at the beginning of the next 2 rows, then 2 (3, 4, 5, 6) stitches at the beginning of the next 2 rows—58 (60, 60, 60, 60) stitches remain.

(Right side) Decrease 1 stitch each side every other row 16 times—26 (28, 28, 28, 28) stitches remain.

(Right side) Bind off 3 stitches at the beginning of the next 4 rows—14 (16, 16, 16, 16) stitches remain.

Bind off the remaining stitches.

FINISHING

Block the pieces to the measurements. Sew the shoulder seams. Set in the Sleeves; sew the side and sleeve seams.

Button Band
With the right side facing, using the smaller needles, pick up and knit 102 (106, 110, 114, 114) stitches along the Left Front edge.

Begin k2, p2 rib; work even for 6 rows.

Bind off all stitches loosely in pattern.

Buttonhole Band
Place markers for 7 buttonholes along the Right Front edge, with the first one ½" (13mm) from the lower edge, the last one ½" (13mm) from the beginning of the neck shaping, and the remaining 5 evenly spaced between.

Work as for the button band for 3 rows.

Buttonhole Row *Work to the marker, [k2tog, yarn over for the buttonhole]; repeat from * for the remaining buttonholes, work to end. Complete as for the button band.

Collar
With the right side facing, using the smaller needles (or the circular needle), beginning at the center of the buttonhole band and ending at the center of the button band, pick up and knit 102 (106, 106, 110, 110) stitches around the neck shaping, including the stitches on the holders.

Begin k2, p2 rib; work even until the collar measures 4½" (11.5cm) from the pickup row.

Bind off all stitches loosely in pattern.

Using the yarn needle, weave in all ends. Sew on the buttons opposite the buttonholes.

Chanel-Style Tweed Jacket

DESIGNED BY JEAN FROST

Coco Chanel brought tweed fabrics into the world of high fashion in the 1950s and 1960s. Unlike the utilitarian garb made throughout the nineteenth and twentieth centuries, which consisted mainly of country-style jackets and capes, the new Chanel designs were couture jackets worn by well-to-do women around the world. Jean's jacket here has the styling and shape of a classic Chanel jacket, but with a rustic look.

INTERMEDIATE

SIZES

Small (Medium, Large, 1X)

KNITTED MEASUREMENTS

Bust 36½ (40½, 45½, 49½)" (92.5 [103, 115.5, 125.5]cm)

Length 21 (22½, 24, 25½)" (53.5 [57, 61, 65]cm), including edging

MATERIALS

4 (5, 5, 6) skeins Tahki Yarns Donegal Tweed (100% pure new wool, 3½ oz [100g], 183 yd [167m]) in #866 grey (MC) and 2 (3, 3, 4) balls in #862 blue (A) (4) medium

1 ball Tahki Yarns Torino (100% extra-fine merino wool, 1¾ oz [50g], 94 yd [86m]) in #106 orange (B) (4) medium

Size 7 (4.5mm) needles, or size needed to obtain gauge

Size 7 (4.5mm) circular needle, 30" (76cm) long (for lower edging)

Split-ring stitch markers

Stitch holders

Yarn needle

9 (9, 9, 11) buttons, ¾" (20mm) in diameter

GAUGE

18 stitches and 24 rows = 4" (10cm) in slip stitch pattern

TAKE TIME TO CHECK GAUGE.

SPECIAL TECHNIQUES

3-Needle Bind-Off Place the stitches of the pieces to be joined on separate needles (or on each end of a circular needle), held one behind the other, with the right sides facing each other, in the left hand.

With a third needle, (the same size or one size larger than the one used for knitting the pieces), knit 2 together (1 stitch from the front needle, 1 stitch from the back needle—1 stitch on the right-hand needle), *knit 2 together (2 stitches on the right-hand needle), bind off 1 stitch in the usual way; repeat from * to the end.

Edge Stitches Knit the first stitch of every row, slip the last stitch of every row purlwise with the yarn in front. Work all shaping after the first and before the last (edge) stitches.

PATTERN STITCHES

Stockinette Stitch
Knit on the right side, purl on the wrong side.

Garter Stitch
Knit every row.

Slip Stitch Pattern

(multiple of 2 stitches + 1 extra stitch)

Note: Slip all stitches purlwise.

Row 1 (right side) Using A, k1 (edge stitch), k1, *slip 1 *with yarn in back*, k1; repeat from * across to the last stitch, slip 1 *with yarn in front* (edge stitch).

Row 2 Using A, k1 (edge stitch), k1, *slip 1 *with yarn in front*, k1; repeat from * across to the last stitch, slip 1 *with yarn in front* (edge stitch).

Rows 3 and 4 Using MC, work even in stockinette stitch, maintaining the edge stitches.

Row 5 Using A, k1 (edge stitch), k2, *slip 1 *with yarn in back*, k1; repeat from * across to the last 2 stitches, k1, slip 1 *with yarn in front* (edge stitch).

Row 6 Using A, k1 (edge stitch), k2, *slip 1 *with yarn in front*, k1; repeat from * across to last 2 stitches, k1, slip 1 *with yarn in front* (edge stitch).

Rows 7 and 8 Repeat rows 3 and 4.

Repeat rows 1–8 for slip stitch pattern.

Note: The Front armholes are longer than those of the Back, moving the shoulder seam to the Back.

SLIP STITCH PATTERN

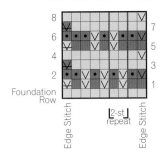

▢	**MC** Knit on right side, purl on wrong side
▪	**Yarn A** Knit on right side, purl on wrong side
▪	**Yarn A** Purl on right side, knit on wrong side
☑	Slip 1 with yarn in back on right side, with yarn in front on wrong side
☑	Slip 1 with yarn in front on right side, with yarn in back on wrong side

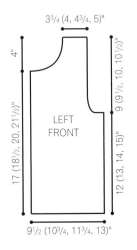

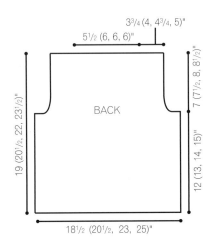

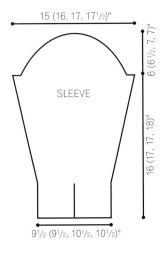

BACK

Using MC, cast on 83 (93, 103, 113) stitches.

(Wrong side) Purl 1 row.

(Right side) Begin slip stitch pattern; changing colors every 2 rows, work even until the piece measures 12 (13, 14, 15)" (30.5 [33, 35.5, 38]cm) from the beginning, ending with (wrong-side) row 2 or 6 of the pattern.

Shape Armhole

(Right side) Bind off 7 (8, 9, 10) stitches at the beginning of the next 2 rows—69 (77, 85, 93) stitches remain.

(Right side) Decrease 1 stitch each side every other row 5 (7, 8, 10) times—59 (63, 69, 73) stitches remain. Work even until the armhole measures 7 (7½, 8, 8½)" (18 [19, 20.5, 21.5]cm) from the beginning of the shaping, ending with (wrong-side) row 2 or 6; place a marker each side of center 25 (27, 27, 27) stitches for the neck.

Shape Neck and Shoulders

(Right side) Work across to the first marker; bind off center stitches; work to end—17 (18, 21, 23) stitches remain each side for the shoulders. Place the remaining stitches on separate holders.

POCKET LININGS (MAKE 2)

Using MC, cast on 23 (23, 25, 27) stitches.

(Right side) Begin stockinette stitch; work even for 17 (17, 19, 19) rows, ending with a right-side row.

Place the stitches on a holder.

LEFT FRONT

Using MC, cast on 43 (49, 53, 59) stitches.

(Wrong side) Purl 1 row.

(Right side) Begin slip stitch pattern; changing colors every 2 rows, work even for 30 rows, ending (wrong-side) row 6 of the pattern.

Join Pockets

(Right side) Continuing in pattern (row 7), k10 (13, 14, 16) stitches; knit next 23 (23, 25, 27) stitches and place on a holder; work to end.

(Wrong side) P10 (13, 14, 16) stitches; purl across the stitches of one Pocket Lining, purl to the end.

Work even until the piece measures 12 (13, 14, 15)" (30.5 [33, 35.5, 38]cm) from the beginning, ending with a wrong-side row.

Shape Armhole

(Right side) At the armhole edge, bind off 7 (8, 9, 10) stitches once—36 (41, 44, 49) stitches remain. Work 1 row even.

(Right side) At the armhole edge, decrease 1 stitch every other row 5 (7, 8, 10) times—31 (34, 36, 39) stitches remain.

Work even until the armhole measures 5 (5½, 6, 6½)" (12.5 [14, 15, 16.5]cm) from the beginning, ending with (right-side) row 3 or 7.

Shape Neck

(Wrong side) Bind off 9 (11, 10, 11) stitches, work to end.

(Right side) At the neck edge (end of the right-side rows), decrease 1 stitch every other row 5 times—17 (18, 21, 23) stitches remain for the shoulder.

Work even until the armhole measures 9 (9½, 10, 10½)" (23 [24, 25.5, 26.5]cm) from the beginning of the shaping, ending with (right-side) row 3 or 7.

Place the stitches on a holder.

RIGHT FRONT

Work as for Left Front, reversing all shaping by working the armhole and shoulder shaping at the beginning of the wrong-side rows and the neck shaping at the beginning of the right-side rows.

CUFFS (MAKE 4)

First Piece

Cast on 22 (22, 24, 24) stitches.

(Wrong side) Purl 1 row.

(Right side) Begin slip stitch pattern, skipping the edge stitch at the beginning of the right-side rows and the end of the wrong-side rows (this will be the center of the cuff); work even for 24 rows, ending with (wrong-side) row 8 of pattern. Place the stitches on a holder.

Second Piece

Cast on and work as for the first piece, skipping the edge stitch at the end of the right-side rows and the beginning of the wrong-side rows (this will be the center of the cuff); do not place the stitches on a holder.

SLEEVES (MAKE 2)

Join Cuffs

(Right side) Continuing in pattern (row 1) on the Second Piece, work across to the last stitch, slip the last stitch to the right-hand needle; place the stitches from the holder (First Piece of the cuff) on the left-hand needle, ready to work a right-side row; return the last stitch of the Second Piece to the left-hand needle; k2tog (last stitch of the Second Piece with first stitch of the First Piece), work to end in pattern—43 (43, 47, 47) stitches, maintaining edge stitches at each side of cuff.

Work even for 1 row.

Shape Sleeve

(Right side) Continuing in pattern, beginning this row, increase 1 stitch each side every 6 (4, 4, 4) rows 12 (15, 15, 16) times, working increased stitches inside the edge stitches, in pattern—67 (73, 77, 79) stitches.

Work even until the piece measures 16 (17, 17, 18)" (40.5 [43, 43, 45.5]cm) from the beginning, ending with (wrong-side) row 2 or 6.

Shape Cap

(Right side) Bind off 7 (8, 9, 10) stitches at the beginning of the next 2 rows—53 (57, 59, 59) stitches remain.

Work even for 2 rows.

(Right side) Decrease 1 stitch each side every other row 15 (17, 18, 18) times—23 stitches remain.

(Right side) Bind off 3 stitches at the beginning of the next 2 rows—17 stitches remain.

Bind off remaining stitches.

FINISHING

Block the pieces to the measurements, being careful not to flatten the texture.

Pocket Edging

Place stitches from the holder onto the needle, ready to work a right-side row.

(Right side) Begin garter stitch; work 4 rows using MC.

(Right side) Change to B; work even for 4 rows, ending with a wrong-side row.

(Right side) Change to A; work 3 rows, ending with a right-side row.

(Wrong side) Continuing with A, bind off all stitches loosely knitwise.

Sew the Pocket neatly to the wrong side of the Front; sew the edging to the right side.

Join the shoulders using the 3-needle bind-off method.

Place a marker at the center of the upper edge of the armhole.

Note: The seam is approximately 1" (2.5cm) from the shoulder edge on the Back.

Centering the Sleeves in the armholes, set in the Sleeves; join the side and sleeve seams.

Neck Band

With the right side facing, using MC and beginning at the Right Front, pick up and knit 83 (87, 87, 89) stitches around the neck shaping.

(Wrong side) Begin garter stitch; work even for 3 rows.

(Right side) Change to B; work even for 4 rows.

(Right side) Change to A; work even for 3 rows, ending with a right-side row.

(Wrong side) Continuing with A, bind off all stitches loosely knitwise.

Lower Edging

With the right side facing, using MC and beginning at the lower left corner, pick up and knit 165 (187, 205, 228) stitches along the entire lower edge across to the Right Front.

(Wrong side) Work as for the neck band.

Lower Sleeve Edging

With the right side facing, using MC and beginning at edge of the cuff slit, pick up and knit 42 (42, 46, 46) stitches around the lower edge of the Sleeve.

(Wrong side) Work as for the neck band.

Cuff Slit Edging

Note: The cuff slit divides the Sleeve in half; edging is worked on the front edge of the slit, then sewn over the back edge of the slit, creating a buttonhole band.

With the right side facing, using MC and beginning at the front edge of the slit, pick up and knit 23 stitches to the lower edge of the Sleeve edging.

(Wrong side) Work as for the Pocket edging, working 2 buttonholes on the third row of B (one 4 stitches from the lower edge, the other 4 stitches from the upper edge). Sew the upper edge of the band to the back of the Sleeve, over the slit.

Button Band

With the right side facing, using MC and beginning at the upper edge of the neck band, pick up and knit 88 (94, 102, 108) stitches along the Left Front to the lower edge.

(Wrong side) Work as for the neck band.

Buttonhole Band

Place markers for 5 (5, 5, 6) buttonholes along the right center Front edge, with the first one 1" (2.5cm) from the lower edge, the last one 1" (2.5cm) from the beginning of the neck shaping, and the remaining 3 (3, 3, 4) evenly spaced between.

(Wrong side) Work as for the Pocket edging, working the buttonholes opposite the markers on the third row of B as follows.

Buttonhole Row *Knit across to 1 stitch before marker, [k2tog, yarn over for the buttonhole]; repeat from * to end.

Using the yarn needle, weave in all ends. Sew on the buttons opposite the buttonholes; 5 (5, 5, 6) on the Left Front and 2 on each Sleeve.

Northern Ireland Peplum Sweater

—— DESIGNED BY GITTA SCHRADE ——

This beauty is basically a simple sweater with interesting finishing details. The pastel shade is a change of pace from the outdoor rustic shades used throughout the rest of this book.

The peplum is worked down once the sweater is complete. The lacy V-neck is finished with a cord tie. Use a combination of pattern instructions and charts to make easy work of the peplum knitting.

EXPERIENCED

SIZES

Small (Medium, Large, X-Large)

KNITTED MEASUREMENTS

Bust 34 (38, 42, 46)" (86 [96.5, 106.5, 117]cm)

Length 18¼ (18¾, 19¼, 19¾)" (46.5 [47.5, 49, 50]cm), excluding peplum (approximately 7" [18cm] long)

MATERIALS

11 (12, 14, 15) balls Tahki Yarns New Tweed (60% wool, 26% viscose, 14% silk, 1¾ oz [50g], 92 yd [84m]) in #048 pink (4) medium

Size 6 (4mm) and size 7 (4.5mm) needles, or size needed to obtain gauge

Size 7 (4.5mm) circular needle, 30" (76cm) long (for Peplum)

Size E-4 (3.5mm) crochet hook (for neck cord)

Waste yarn (for provisional cast-on)

Several yards (meters) ravel cord (crochet cotton or other smooth, thin nylon cord, or cotton yarn for provisional cast-on)

Stitch markers

Stitch holders

Yarn needle

GAUGE

18 stitches and 24 rows = 4" (10cm) in stockinette stitch, using the larger needles

TAKE TIME TO CHECK GAUGE.

ABBREVIATIONS AND TERMS

k1-f/b Knit next stitch, do not drop from left-hand needle, knit the same stitch through the back loop, drop stitch from left-hand needle—1 stitch increased.

M1 (Make 1 increase) Lift the strand between the needles to the left-hand needle and work the strand through the back loop, twisting it to prevent a hole, [knit or purl as indicated by pattern stitch].

s2kp (double centered decrease) Slip 2 stitches together knitwise (as if to knit them together) to right-hand needle, k1, pass both slipped stitches together over the knit stitch.

SPECIAL TECHNIQUE

Provisional Cast-On

Step 1 Using the larger needles and smooth waste yarn, cast on half the number of stitches needed, plus 2 extra to be safe.

Note: The waste yarn will be removed when beginning the peplum, so any extra stitches may be left unworked.

Lace Pattern for Peplum

(worked over 15 stitches; see chart)

Row 1 (right side) Yo, ssk, k1, yo, ssk, k5, k2tog, yo, k1, k2tog, yo.

Row 2 and all wrong-side rows Purl all stitches and yarn overs.

Row 3 K1, yo, ssk, k1, yo, ssk, k3, k2tog, yo, k1, k2tog, yo, k1.

Row 5 K2, yo, ssk, k1, yo, ssk, k1, k2tog, yo, k1, k2tog, yo, k2.

Row 7 K3, yo, ssk, k1, yo, s2kp, yo, k1, k2tog, yo, k3.

Row 9 K4, yo, ssk, k3, k2tog, yo, k4.

Row 11 K5, yo, ssk, k1, k2tog, yo, k5.

Row 13 K6, yo, s2kp, yo, k6.

Row 14 Repeat row 2.

Repeat rows 1–14 for lace pattern.

Step 2 K1-f/b in each stitch across, as needed, to end with the correct number of cast-on stitches specified in the instructions.

Step 3 Work 3 rows even in stockinette stitch.

Step 4 Knit 1 row with ravel cord (crochet cotton or other thin, smooth yarn or cord).

Step 5 Change to garment yarn; begin working the piece as specified in the instructions.

Step 6 When ready to begin the peplum, insert the circular needle into each garment stitch above the row of ravel cord, and pull on the ravel cord to separate the garment piece from the waste yarn; there are now live stitches on the circular needle to begin working the peplum. Continue as instructed.

Note: At seams, it may be necessary to pick up an extra stitch or work 2 stitches together to obtain the correct number of stitches in step 6. Or, the stitch count may be adjusted on the first row following the pickup row.

PATTERN STITCHES

Stockinette Stitch
Knit on the right side, purl on the wrong side.

Garter Stitch
Knit every row.

Chain
Wrap the yarn around the hook (yarn over), and draw it through the loop on the hook to form the first chain.

Seed Stitch
(multiple of 2 stitches + 1)

Row 1 K1, * pl, k1; repeat from * to end.

Row 2 Knit the purl stitches and purl the knit stitches as they appear.

Repeat row 2 for seed stitch.

LACE CHART (Peplum)

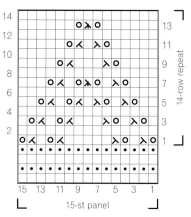

☐ Knit on right side, purl on wrong side	⊼ K2tog
• Purl on right side, knit on wrong side	⋋ Ssk
○ Yo	⋌ S2kp
	⊠ M1

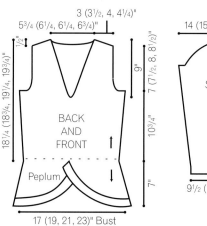

BACK AND FRONT

Peplum

3 (3½, 4, 4¼)"
5¾ (6¼, 6¼, 6¾)"
½"
9"
7 (7½, 8, 8½)"
18¼ (18¾, 19¼, 19¾)"
10¾"
7"
17 (19, 21, 23)" Bust
14 (16¼, 18½, 20¼)" Waist

SLEEVE

14 (15, 15¾, 16¾)"
4 (4½, 4¾, 5)"
17 (17½, 18, 18)"
9½ (10, 10½, 11)"

BACK

Using the larger needles, cast on 63 (73, 83, 91) stitches.

Note: The peplum will be worked downward from this edge; use the provisional cast-on (see Special Technique; or use size 9 needles to cast on, creating a loose cast-on edge to pick up stitches for the peplum).

(Wrong side) Begin stockinette stitch; work even for 7 rows, ending with a wrong-side row.

Shape Sides

(Right side) Beginning this row, increase 1 stitch each side every 8 rows 7 times—77 (87, 97, 105) stitches.

Work even until the piece measures 10¾" (27.5cm) from the beginning, ending with a wrong-side row.

Shape Armhole

(Right side) Bind off 3 (3, 4, 5) stitches at beginning of next 2 rows, then 2 stitches at beginning of next 2 (2, 4, 4) rows—67 (77, 81, 87) stitches remain.

(Right side) Decrease 1 stitch each side every other row 2 (4, 4, 5) times—63 (69, 73, 77) stitches remain.

Work even until the armhole measures 6½ (7, 7½, 8)" (16.5 [18, 19, 20.5]cm) from the beginning of the shaping, ending with a wrong-side row; place a marker each side of the center 17 (19, 19, 21) stitches.

Shape Neck

(Right side) Work across to the marker; join a second ball of yarn and bind off the center stitches, work to end.

Working both sides at the same time, at each neck edge bind off 5 stitches once, then 4 stitches once—14 (16, 18, 19) stitches remain each side for the shoulders after the neck shaping is completed; AT THE SAME TIME, on the last row of neck shaping (the right neck edge is completed; the left will be completed on the next row), end with a wrong-side row.

Shape Shoulders

(Right side) Bind off 7 (8, 9, 10) stitches at beginning of next 2 rows, then 7 (8, 9, 9) stitches at beginning of next 2 rows.

FRONT

Note: The neck shaping begins before the side shaping is completed or before the armhole shaping begins (or both) on all except the largest size. Read the instructions carefully for your size.

Using the larger needles, cast on 63 (73, 83, 91) stitches. (See the note for Back.)

(Wrong side) Begin stockinette stitch; work even for 7 rows, ending with a wrong-side row.

Shape Sides

(Right side) Beginning this row, increase 1 stitch each side every 8 rows 7 times as for the Back; AT THE SAME TIME, when the piece measures 9¼ (9¾, 10¼, 10¾)" (23 [25, 26, 27.5]cm) from the beginning, end with a wrong-side row; place a marker on the center stitch.

Note: Complete the side shaping, if necessary, for your size; then work the armhole shaping as for the Back and, AT THE SAME TIME, work the neck shaping.

Shape Neck

(Right side) Work across to 4 stitches before the marked stitch, k2tog, k2 (left Front); place the center stitch on a holder; join a second ball of yarn, k2, ssk, work to end (right Front). Work 1 row even.

(Right side) Decrease 1 stitch each neck edge in this way, alternately [(every other row) twice, every 4 rows once—3 stitches decreased each neck edge every 8 rows] until 17 (18, 18, 19) stitches have been decreased—14 (16, 18, 19) stitches remain each shoulder.

Work even until the armhole measures the same as the Back to the shoulder shaping, ending with a wrong-side row.

Shape Shoulders

(Right side) Bind off 7 (8, 9, 10) stitches at beginning of next 2 rows, then 7 (8, 9, 9) stitches at beginning of next 2 rows.

SLEEVES (MAKE 2)

Using the smaller needles, cast on 43 (45, 47, 49) stitches.

(Right side) Begin seed stitch; work even for 8 rows, ending with a wrong-side row.

(Right side) Change to the larger needles and stockinette stitch; work even for 8 rows, ending with a wrong-side row.

Shape Sleeves

(Right side) Beginning this row, increase 1 stitch each side every 10 rows 3 (1, 1, 1) time(s), then every 8 (8, 8, 7) rows 7 (10, 11, 12) times—63 (67, 71, 75) stitches.

Work even until the piece measures 17 (17½, 18, 18)" (43 [44.5, 45.5, 45.5]cm) from the beginning, ending with a wrong-side row.

Shape Cap

(Right side) Bind off 3 (3, 4, 5) stitches at beginning of next 2 rows, then 2 stitches at beginning of next 4 rows.

(Right side) Decrease 1 stitch each side every other row 5 (6, 7, 8) times, then every row 4 times.

Bind off 4 stitches at beginning of next 4 rows—15 (17, 17, 17) stitches remain.

Bind off the remaining stitches.

FINISHING

Block the pieces to the measurements. Sew the shoulder and side seams; place a marker in the center stitch of the Front at the lower edge.

Peplum

Note: The circular needle is used for ease in working the peplum. Do not join; instead, work back and forth in rows.

With the right side facing, using the circular needle, pick up (live stitches from the provisional cast-on, if used) at the lower edge of the Front and Back in this way: slip 7 (7, 8, 8) stitches before the marked center stitch to the needle, slip the center stitch, then the remaining stitches of the Front to the needle, place a marker at the side seam; slip all stitches of the Back to the needle, place a marker at the side seam; slip the remaining Front stitches onto the needle; cast on 14 (14, 16, 16) stitches—140 (160, 182, 198) stitches.

(Wrong side) Begin garter stitch; work even for 3 rows, ending with a wrong-side row.

Begin Lace Pattern

Note: The peplum shaping chart shows stitches for the smallest size only; use the chart only as a reference *for increases and decreases at the beginning of right-side rows, referring to the written text for the actual number of stitches to work before the first lace panel; this shaping will be mirrored at the end of these rows (see the written instructions). Row 3 (increase row) will have additional increases worked across the row, besides those shown on the chart (refer to the written instructions).*

Row 1 (right side) K1, ssk, k16 (19, 23, 25), place a marker; referring to the written instructions or chart, work row 1 of lace pattern across the next 15 stitches, place a marker; k5 (7, 9, 11), slip the side-seam marker, k5 (7, 9, 11), place a marker; work lace pattern across the next 15 stitches, place a marker; [k4 (7, 10, 12), place a marker; work lace pattern across the next 15 stitches, place a marker] twice; k5 (7, 9, 11), slip the side-seam marker, k5 (7, 9, 11), place a marker; work lace pattern across the next 15 stitches, place a marker; k15 (18, 22, 24), k2tog, k1—138 (158, 180, 196) stitches remain.

Rows 2 and 4 Purl.

Row 3 K1, ssk, k14 (17, 21, 23), M1, k1; 15 stitches in lace pattern; k5 (7, 9, 11) (side seam), M1, k5 (7, 9, 11); 15 stitches in lace pattern; [k2 (3, 5, 6), M1, k2 (4, 5, 6); 15 stitches in lace pattern] twice; k5 (7, 9, 11) (side seam), M1, k5 (7, 9, 11); 15 stitches in lace pattern; k1, M1, k13 (16, 20, 22), k2tog, k1—142 (162, 184, 200) stitches.

Row 5 K1, [ssk] twice, k13 (16, 20, 22); 15 stitches in lace pattern; k11 (15, 19, 23); 15 stitches in lace pattern; [k5 (8, 11, 13); 15 stitches in lace pattern] twice; k11 (15, 19, 23); 15 stitches in lace pattern; k12 (15, 19, 21), [k2tog] twice, k1—138 (158, 180, 196) stitches remain.

Row 6 Repeat row 2.

Continuing in this way (rows 1–6), decrease 1 stitch each side every other row twice (as rows 1 and 3), then 2 stitches each side every other row once (as row 5—8 stitches decrease over 6 rows) and, AT THE SAME TIME, increase 6 stitches (as row 3) every 6 rows, until a total of 3 increase rows have been worked—134 (154, 176, 192) stitches remain.

Continue lace pattern until 28 rows (2 repeats of the 14-row lace pattern) have been completed; AT THE SAME TIME, on right-side rows, decrease 2 stitches each side every other row twice, then 1 stitch each side every other row once (10 stitches decrease over 6 rows), and increase 6 stitches (as row 3) on row 21 of the lace pattern.

Then, on right-side rows, decrease 2 stitches each side every other row twice and increase 6 stitches on row 25 of the lace pattern—128 (148, 170, 186) stitches remain.

Work even until 28 rows of the lace pattern are completed.

Begin stockinette stitch on all stitches.

Shape Peplum Ends

Bind off 4 stitches at the beginning of the next 6 rows, then 6 stitches at the beginning of the next 2 (2, 4, 4) rows—92 (112, 122, 138) stitches remain.

Place the stitches on a holder or waste yarn.

Peplum Edging

With the right side facing, using the circular needle, pick up and knit 55 (55, 60, 62) stitches up the shaped peplum edge; knit 92 (112, 122, 138) stitches from the holder, decreasing 1 stitch at the center Back; pick up and knit 55 (55, 60, 62) stitches down the shaped peplum edge—201 (221, 241, 261) stitches.

Next Row (wrong side) Purl all stitches.

Row 1 (right side) [K1, yo, ssk, k5, k2tog, yo] 20 (22, 24, 26) times, k1.

Rows 2, 4, 6, and 8 Purl, increasing 1 stitch each side.

Row 3 K1, [k2, yo, ssk, k3, k2tog, yo, k1] 20 (22, 24, 26) times, k2.

Row 5 K2, [k3, yo, ssk, k1, k2tog, yo, k2] 20 (22, 24, 26) times, k3.

Row 7 K3, [k4, yo, s2kp, yo, k3] 20 (22, 24, 26) times, k4.

Row 9 K4, [k1, yo, k9, yo] 20 (22, 24, 26) times, k5—241 (265, 289, 313) stitches.

Change to seed stitch; work even for 2 rows.

Bind off all stitches loosely in pattern.

Sew the cast-on stitches of the peplum behind the center stitches.

Neck Band

With the right side facing, using the circular needle and beginning at the left shoulder seam, pick up and knit 42 stitches down the left Front neck shaping; knit the center stitch from holder; pick up and knit 42 stitches up the right Front neck shaping to the shoulder seam, 40 stitches across the back neck—125 stitches.

Round 1 (right side) [K1, yo, ssk, k5, k2tog, yo] 4 times; k1, s2kp (center Front) k1; [k1, yo, ssk, k5, k2tog, yo] 8 times.

Rounds 2–8 Continue in pattern from the chart, working double centered decrease (s2kp) at the center Front every other row, as shown.

Begin seed stitch; work 2 rounds, continuing s2kp at the center Front.

Bind off all stitches loosely in pattern, working s2kp at the center Front on the bind-off row.

Set in the Sleeves; sew the sleeve seams.

NECK CORD

Using the crochet hook, work a chain 48" (122cm) long.

Thread the cord through the eyelets on the neck band.

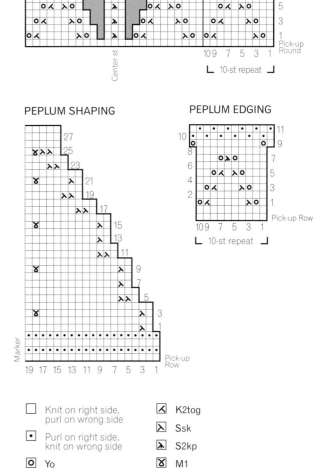

NECK BAND

PEPLUM SHAPING

PEPLUM EDGING

	Knit on right side, purl on wrong side		K2tog
	Purl on right side, knit on wrong side		Ssk
	Yo		S2kp
			M1
			No stitch

Outer Hebrides Sampler Throw

DESIGNED BY NANCY J. THOMAS

I had always dreamed of an extraordinary throw covered in leaf stitches. One big love of mine is basket-weave stitches, and these woven-looking patterns seemed like the perfect way to ground a leaf-stitch sampler. As I developed my vision for this book, I pictured tweed yarn and stitches in a natural setting. I framed the center four panels with a neutral border and put the color emphasis on the center stitches. For a final touch, I added a leafy border on the two short sides. Knit side to side, the border makes a great car-knitting project.

EXPERIENCED

KNITTED MEASUREMENTS

Approximately 40" wide x 54" long (101.5cm x 137cm), excluding leaf edging

MATERIALS

1 skein Tahki Yarns Donegal Tweed (100% pure new wool, 3½ oz [100g], 183 yd [167m]) in #849 medium eggplant (A), 3 skeins in #866 medium gray (B), 2 skeins in #867 taupe (C), and 1 skein each in #892 green (D), #893 pumpkin (E), #846 gold (F), and #818 pink (G) (4) medium

Size 9 (5.5mm) needles, or size needed to obtain gauge

Cable needle

Stitch markers

Stitch holders

Yarn needle

GAUGE

15 stitches and 26 rows = 4" (10cm) in double seed stitch

TAKE TIME TO CHECK GAUGE.

ABBREVIATIONS AND TERMS

M1 (make 1 increase) Lift the strand between the needles to the left-hand needle and work the strand through the back loop, twisting it to prevent a hole, [knit or purl as indicated by pattern stitch].

psso (pass slip stitch over knit stitch)

PATTERN STITCHES
(see charts)

Stockinette Stitch
Knit on the right side, purl on the wrong side.

Reverse Stockinette Stitch
Purl on the right side, knit on the wrong side.

Garter Stitch
Knit every row.

Double Seed Stitch
(even number of stitches)
Rows 1 (right side) and 2 (wrong side) *K1, p1; repeat from * across.
Rows 3 and 4 *P1, k1; repeat from * across.
Repeat rows 1–4 for double seed stitch.

DOUBLE SEED

4 ⋅ 3
2 ⋅ 1

⌊2-st⌋
repeat

☐ Knit on right side, purl on wrong side

⊡ Purl on right side, knit on wrong side

Stockinette Basket Weave

(multiple of 8 stitches + 2 extra stitches)

Rows 1 and 3 (wrong side) K4, *p2, k6; repeat from *across to the last 6 stitches, end p2, k4.

Row 2 P4, k2, *p6, k2; repeat from * across to the last 4 stitches, p4.

Row 4 Knit.

Rows 5 and 7 K8, *p2, k6; repeat from * across, end last repeat k8.

Row 6 P8, *k2, p6; repeat from * across, end last repeat p8.

Row 8 Knit.

Repeat rows 1–8 for stockinette basket weave.

STOCKINETTE BASKET WEAVE

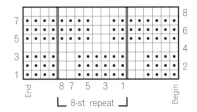

☐ Knit on right side, purl on wrong side

▪ Purl on right side, knit on wrong side

Garter Stitch Basket Weave (multiple of 10 stitches)

Rows 1, 3, and 5 (right side) *[K1, p1] twice, k6; repeat from * to end.

Rows 2, 4, and 6 *K5, [p1, k1] twice, p1; repeat from * to end.

Rows 7–8 Knit.

Rows 9, 11, and 13 *K6, [p1, k1] twice; repeat from * to end.

Rows 10, 12, and 14 *[P1, k1] twice, p1, k5; repeat from * to end.

Rows 15–16 Knit.

Repeat rows 1–16 for garter stitch basket weave.

GARTER STITCH BASKET WEAVE

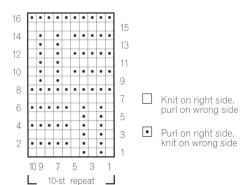

☐ Knit on right side, purl on wrong side

▪ Purl on right side, knit on wrong side

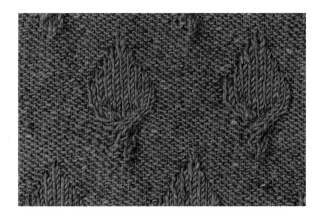

Cable Leaf

(multiple of 18 stitches + 9 extra stitches)

C5B (5-stitch right cable) Slip 3 stitches onto a cable needle and hold to the back, knit 2 stitches, knit 3 stitches from the cable needle.

C4B (4-stitch right cable) Slip 2 stitches onto a cable needle and hold to the back, knit 2 stitches, knit 2 stitches from the cable needle.

C4F (4-stitch left cable) Slip 2 stitches onto a cable needle and hold to the front, knit 2 stitches, knit 2 stitches from the cable needle.

Row 1 (right side) *P4, k1, p13; repeat from * across, end last repeat p4.

Row 2 and all wrong-side rows Knit the knit stitches and purl the purl stitches as they face you.

Row 3 *P3, k3, p12; repeat from * across, end last repeat p3.

Row 5 *P2, k5, p11; repeat from * across, end last repeat p2.

Row 7 *P2, C5B, p11; repeat from * across, end last repeat p2.

Row 9 *C4B, k1, C4F, p9; repeat from * across to the last 9 stitches, end C4B, k1, C4F.

Rows 11 and 13 *K9, p9; repeat from * across to the last 9 stitches, end k9.

Row 15 *P1, k7, p10; repeat from * across, end last repeat p1.

Row 17 Repeat row 5.

Row 19 Repeat row 3.

Row 21 Repeat row 1.

Row 23 *P13, k1, p4; repeat from * across, end last repeat p13.

Row 25 *P12, k3, p3; repeat from * across, end last repeat p12.

Row 27 *P11, k5, p2; repeat from * across, end last repeat p11.

Row 29 *P11, C5B, p2; repeat from * across, end last repeat p11.

Row 31 *P9, C4B, k1, C4F; repeat from * across to last 9 stitches, end p9.

Rows 33 and 35 *P9, k9; repeat from * across to last 9 stitches, end p9.

Row 37 *P10, k7, p1; repeat from * across, end last repeat p10.

Row 39 Repeat row 27.

Row 41 Repeat row 25.

Row 43 Repeat row 23.

Row 44 Repeat row 2.

Repeat rows 1–44 for cable leaf.

CABLE LEAF

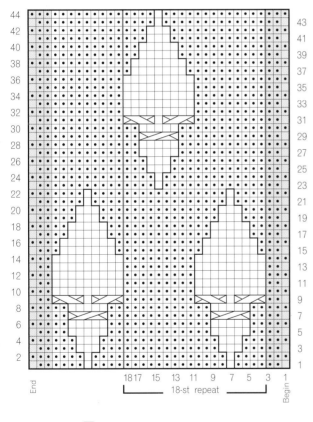

☐ Edge stitches

☐ Knit on right side, purl on wrong side

⊡ Purl on right side, knit on wrong side

⊠ C5B

⊠ C4B

⊠ C4F

Vine Leaf (multiple of 26 stitches)

k1-f/b Knit next stitch, do not drop from left-hand needle, knit the same stitch through the back loop, drop stitch from left-hand needle—1 stitch increased.

p1-f/b Purl next stitch, do not drop from left-hand needle, purl the same stitch through the back loop, drop stitch from left-hand needle—1 stitch increased..

dc-dec Slip 2 stitches together knitwise to the right-hand needle, k1, pass two slipped stitches over knit stitch.

Note: Stitch count varies.

Row 1 (wrong side) *K5, p5, k4, p3, k9; repeat from * to end.

Row 2 *P7, p2tog, k1-f/b, k2, p4, k2, yo, k1, yo, k2, p5; repeat from * to end.

Row 3 *K5, p7, k4, p2, k1, p1, k8; repeat from * to end.

Row 4 *P6, p2tog, k1, p1-f/b, k2, p4, k3, yo, k1, yo, k3, p5; repeat from * to end.

Row 5 *K5, p9, k4, p2, k2, p1, k7; repeat from * to end.

Row 6 *P5, p2tog, k1, p1-f/b, p1, k2, p4, ssk, k5, k2tog, p5; repeat from * to end.

Row 7 *K5, p7, k4, p2, k3, p1, k6; repeat from * to end.

Row 8 *P4, p2tog, k1, p1-f/b, p2, k2, p4, ssk, k3, k2tog, p5; repeat from * to end.

Row 9 *K5, p5, k4, p2, k4, p1, k5; repeat from * to end.

Row 10 P5, yo, k1, yo, p4, k2, p4, ssk, k1, k2tog, p5; repeat from * to end.

Row 11 *K5, p3, k4, p2, k4, p3, k5; repeat from * to end.

Row 12 *P5, [k1, yo] twice, k1, p4, k1, M1, k1, p2tog, p2, dc-dec, p5; repeat from * to end.

Row 13 *K9, p3, k4, p5, k5; repeat from * to end.

Row 14 *P5, k2, yo, k1, yo, k2, p4, k1, k1-f/b, k1, p2tog, p7; repeat from * to end.

Row 15 *K8, p1, k1, p2, k4, p7, k5; repeat from * to end.

Row 16 *P5, k3, yo, k1, yo, k3, p4, k2, p1-f/b, k1, p2tog, p6; repeat from * to end.

Row 17 *K7, p1, k2, p2, k4, p9, k5; repeat from * to end.
Row 18 *P5, ssk, k5, k2tog, p4, k2, p1, p1-f/b, k1, p2tog, p5; repeat from * to end.
Row 19 *K6, p1, k3, p2, k4, p7, k5; repeat from * to end.
Row 20 *P5, ssk, k3, k2tog, p4, k2, p2, p1-f/b, k1, p2tog, p4; repeat from * to end.
Row 21 *K5, p1, k4, p2, k4, p5, k5; repeat from * to end.
Row 22 *P5, ssk, k1, k2tog, p4, k2, p4, yo, k1, yo, p5; repeat from * to end.
Row 23 *K5, p3, k4, p2, k4, p3, k5; repeat from * to end.
Row 24 *P5, dc-dec, p2, p2tog, k1, M1, k1, p4, [k1, yo] twice, k1, p5; repeat from * to end.
Repeat rows 1–24 for vine leaf.

ENCASED LEAVES

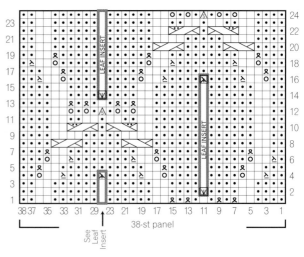

VINE LEAF
Stitch count varies

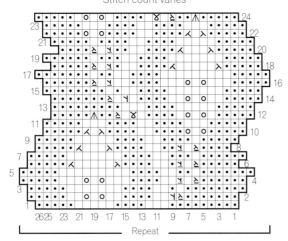

Repeat

	Knit on wrong side, purl on right side		Yo
•	Purl on wrong side, knit on right side		Ssk
	P2tog		K2tog
	K1-f/b		M1
	P1-f/b		Dc-dec

	Knit on wrong side, purl on right side		S2kp
•	Purl on wrong side, knit on right side		4-st decrease
	K1-tbl		C4B
	Dc-inc		C4F
	P2tog		C4pB
	Yo		C4pF

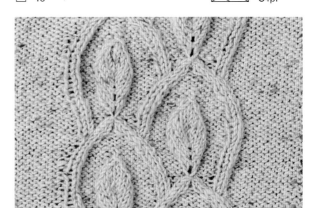

LEAF INSERT
(Encased Leaves)

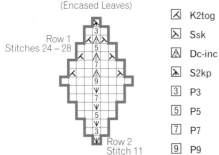

Row 1
Stitches 24 – 28

Row 2
Stitch 11

	K2tog
	Ssk
	Dc-inc
	S2kp
3	P3
5	P5
7	P7
9	P9

Encased Leaves (panel of 38 stitches)
Note: Stitch count varies.

Leaf Insert Work the stitches for the leaves as shown on the leaf insert chart, where indicated on the main chart; leaf instructions are noted in written instructions within angled brackets (< >).

K1-tbl Knit next stitch through the back loop.

C4B (4-stitch right cable) Slip 2 stitches onto a cable needle and hold to the back, knit 2 stitches, knit 2 stitches from the cable needle.

C4F (4-stitch left cable) Slip 2 stitches onto a cable needle and hold to the front, knit 2 stitches, knit 2 stitches from the cable needle.

C4pB (4-stitch right purl cable) Slip 2 stitches onto a cable needle and hold to the back, knit 2 stitches, purl 2 stitches from the cable needle.

C4pF (4-stitch left purl cable) Slip 2 stitches onto a cable needle and hold to the front, purl 2 stitches, knit 2 stitches from the cable needle.

dc-inc (double centered increase) Knit into the back of the stitch in the row below; knit into the back loop of the stitch on the left-hand needle; using the left-hand needle, pick up the left-side strand of the same stitch in the row below and knit 1 through the back loop in this strand to make a third stitch.

s2kp (double centered decrease) Slip 2 stitches together knitwise (as if to knit them together) to right-hand needle, k1, pass both slipped stitches together over the knit stitch.

4-st dec (4-stitch decrease) Ssk, knit 3 together, pass ssk stitches over knit 3 together stitches.

Row 1 (wrong side) K2, p2, k6, <p5>, k6, p2, [k1-tbl, k1] twice, p1, [k1, k1-tbl] twice, p2, k4.

Row 2 P4, k2, p4, <dc-inc>, p4, k2, p6, <ssk, k1, k2tog>, p6, k2, p2.

Row 3 K2, p2, k6, <p3>, k6, p2, k4, <p3>, k4, p2, k4.

Row 4 P2, p2tog, k2, yo, p4, <k1, dc-inc, k1>, p4, yo, k2, p2tog, p4, <s2kp>, p4, p2tog, k2, yo, p2.

Row 5 K2, k1-tbl, p2, k11, p2, k1-tbl, k4, <p5>, k4, k1-tbl, p2, k3.

Row 6 P1, p2tog, k2, yo, p5, <k2, dc-inc, k2>, p5, yo, k2, p2tog, p7, p2tog, k2, yo, p3.

Row 7 K3, k1-tbl, p2, k9, p2, k1-tbl, k5, <p7>, k5, k1-tbl, p2, k2.

Row 8 P2, k2, p6, <k3, dc-inc, k3>, p6, C4F, p5, C4B, p4.

Row 9 K4, p4, k5, p4, k6, <p9>, k6, p2, k2.

Row 10 P2, k2, p6, <ssk, k5, k2tog>, p6, k2, C4pF, p1, C4pB, k2, p4.

Row 11 K4, p2, k2, p2, k1, p2, k2, p2, k6, <p7>, k6, p2, k2.

Row 12 P2, k2, p6, <ssk, k3, k2tog>, p6, k2, [yo, p1] twice, 4-st dec, [p1, yo] twice, k2, p4.

Row 13 K4, p2, [k1-tbl, k1] twice, p1, [k1, k1-tbl] twice, p2, k6, <p5>, k6, p2, k2.

Row 14 P2, k2, p6, <ssk, k1, k2tog>, p6, k2, p4, <dc-inc>, p4, k2, p4.

Row 15 K4, p2, k4, <p3>, k4, p2, k6, <p3>, k6, p2, k2.

Row 16 P2, yo, k2, p2tog, p4, <s2kp>, p4, p2tog, k2, yo, p4, <k1, dc-inc, k1>, p4, yo, k2, p2tog, p2.

Row 17 K3, p2, k1-tbl, k4, <p5>, k4, k1-tbl, p2, k11, p2, k1-tbl, k2.

Row 18 P3, yo, k2, p2tog, p7, p2tog, k2, yo, p5, <k2, dc-inc, k2>, p5, yo, k2, p2tog, p1.

Row 19 K2, p2, k1-tbl, k5, <p7>, k5, k1-tbl, p2, k9, p2, k1-tbl, k3.

Row 20 P4, C4F, p5, C4B, p6, <k3, dc-inc, k3>, p6, k2, p2.

Row 21 K2, p2, k6, <p9>, k6, p4, k5, p4, k4.

Row 22 P4, k2, C4pF, p1, C4pB, k2, p6, <ssk, k5, k2tog>, p6, k2, p2.

Row 23 K2, p2, k6, <p7>, k6, p2, k2, p2, k1, p2, k2, p2, k4.

Row 24 P4, k2, [yo, p1] twice, 4-st dec, [p1, yo] twice, k2, p6, <ssk, k3, k2tog>, p6, k2, p2.

Repeat rows 1–24 for encased leaves.

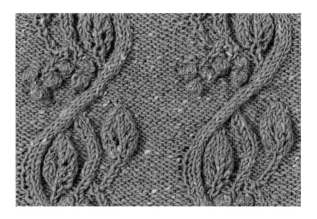

Bobble Leaves (panel of 21 stitches)
Note: Stitch count varies.

Leaf Insert Work the stitches for the leaves as shown on the leaf insert chart, where indicated on the main chart; leaf instructions are noted in the written instructions within arrow brackets (< >).

C3pB (3-stitch right purl cable) Slip 1 stitch onto a cable needle and hold to the back, knit 2 stitches, purl 1 stitch from the cable needle.

C3pF (3-stitch left purl cable) Slip 2 stitches onto a cable needle and hold to the front, purl 1 stitch, knit 2 stitches from the cable needle.

C4pB (4-stitch right purl cable) Slip 1 stitch onto a cable needle and hold to the back, knit 3 stitches, purl 1 stitch from the cable needle.

C4pF (4-stitch left purl cable) Slip 3 stitches onto a cable needle and hold to the front, purl 1 stitch, knit 3 stitches from the cable needle.

C5pB (5-stitch right purl cable) Slip 2 stitches onto a cable needle and hold to the back, knit 3 stitches, purl 2 stitches from the cable needle.

C5pF (5-stitch left purl cable) Slip 3 stitches onto a cable needle and hold to the front, purl 2 stitches, knit 3 stitches from the cable needle.

MB (make bobble) [Knit into the front loop then the back loop] of the next stitch twice (make 4 stitches in

one); turn, purl 4 stitches; turn, ssk, k2tog, slip the
2 stitches just made to the left-hand needle, k2tog—
1 stitch remains.

inc-4 (make 5 stitches in one) M1, yo, k1, yo, M1.

Tw2L (left twist) Skip the first stitch on the left-hand
needle; knit the next stitch through the back loop,
leaving the stitch on the left-hand needle; knit the
skipped stitch through the front loop; slip both stitches
off the left-hand needle.

Tw2R (right twist) Knit 2 stitches together, leaving the
stitches on the left-hand needle; knit the first stitch
again; slip both stitches off the left-hand needle.

Tw2pL (2-stitch left purl twist) Slip 1 stitch onto a cable
needle and hold to the front, purl 1 stitch, knit 1 stitch
from the cable needle.

Tw2pR (2-stitch right purl twist) Slip 1 stitch onto a
cable needle and hold to the back, knit 1 stitch, purl 1
stitch from the cable needle.

Tw3pL (3-stitch left purl twist) Slip 1 stitch onto a cable
needle and hold to the front, purl 2 stitches, knit 1 stitch
from the cable needle.

Tw3pR (3-stitch right purl twist) Slip 2 stitches onto a
cable needle and hold to the back, knit 1 stitch, purl 2
stitches from the cable needle.

Row 1 (right side) P5, C5pB, p7, MB, p3.

Row 2 and all wrong-side rows Knit the knit stitches,
bobbles and k3tog at the top of the leaf, purl the purl
stitches as they face you.

Row 3 P3, C5pB, p2, MB, p4, MB, Tw2pR, MB, p2.

Row 5 P2, C4pB, k1, p2, MB, Tw2pL, MB, p2, Tw2pR, p4.

Row 7 P1, C4pB, p1, Tw2pL, p2, Tw2pR, p1, C3pB, p5.

Row 9 C4pB, p3, <inc-4>, p2, Tw2pL, Tw2pR, Tw3pL, p4.

Row 11 K3, p4, <k2, yo, k1, yo, k2>, p3, Tw2L, p3,
Tw2pL, p3.

Row 13 K3, p4, <ssk, k1, yo, k1, yo, k1, k2tog>, p3,
C3pF, p3, Tw2pL, p2.

Row 15 C4pF, p3, <ssk, k3, k2tog>, p4, C3pF, p3,
<inc-4>, p2.

Row 17 P1, C4pF, p2, <ssk, k1, k2tog>, p5, k2, p3,
<k2, yo, k1, yo, k2>, p2.

Row 19 P2, C4pF, p1, <k3tog>, p4, C3pB, p3, <ssk,
k1, yo, k1, yo, k1, k2tog>, p2.

Row 21 P3, C5pF, p3, C3pB, p4, <ssk, k3, k2tog>, p2.

Row 23 P5, C5pF, C3pB, p5, <ssk, k1, k2tog>, p2.

Row 25 P7, C5pF, p6, <k3tog>, p2.

Row 27 P9, C5pF, p7.

Row 29 P3, MB, p7, C5pF, p5.

Row 31 P2, MB, Tw2pL, MB, p4, MB, p2, C5pF, p3.

BOBBLE LEAVES
Stitch count varies

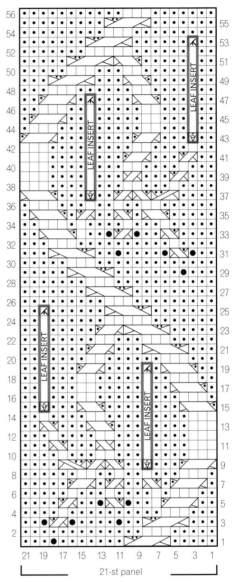

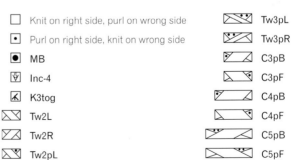

☐ Knit on right side, purl on wrong side		Tw3pL
• Purl on right side, knit on wrong side		Tw3pR
● MB		C3pB
Inc-4		C3pF
K3tog		C4pB
Tw2L		C4pF
Tw2R		C5pB
Tw2pL		C5pF
Tw2pR		

Row 33 P4, Tw2pL, p2, MB, Tw2pR, MB, p2, k1, C4pF, p2.

Row 35 P5, C3pF, p1, Tw2pL, p2, Tw2pR, p1, C4pF, p1.

Row 37 P4, Tw3pR, Tw2pL, Tw2pR, p2, <inc-4>, p3, C4pF.

Row 39 P3, Tw2pR, p3, Tw2R, p3, <k2, yo, k1, yo, k2>, p4, k3.

Row 41 P2, Tw2pR, p3, C3pB, p3, <ssk, k1, yo, k1, yo, k1, k2tog>, p4, k3.

Row 43 P2, <inc-4>, p3, C3pB, p4, <ssk, k3, k2tog>, p3, C4pB.

Row 45 P2, <k2, yo, k1, yo, k2>, p3, k2, p5, <ssk, k1, k2tog>, p2, C4pB, p1.

Row 47 P2, <ssk, k1, yo, k1, yo, k1, k2tog>, p3, C3pF, p4, <k3tog>, p1, C4pB, p2.

Row 49 P2, <ssk, k3, k2tog>, p4, C3pF, p3, C5pB, p3.

Row 51 P2, <ssk, k1, k2tog>, p5, C3pF, C5pB, p5.

Row 53 P2, <k3tog>, p6, C5pB, p7.

Row 55 P7, C5pB, p9.

Row 56 Repeat row 2.

Repeat rows 1–56 for bobble leaves.

LEAF INSERT
(Bobble Leaves)

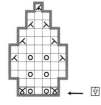

⬓	Ssk
⬓	K2tog
⊠	M1
◻	Yo
⬓	K3tog

SIDE PANELS (MAKE 2)

Corner Block

Using A, cast on 34 stitches.

(Wrong side) Knit 1 row.

(Right side) Begin double seed stitch; work even until the piece measures 9" (23cm) from the beginning, ending with a wrong-side row.

Fasten off A; join B.

Center Block

(Right side) Using B, knit 1 row.

(Wrong side) Begin stockinette basket weave; work even until the piece measures 45" (114cm) from the beginning (center section measures 36" [91cm]), ending with a right-side row.

Fasten off B; join A.

Corner Block

(Wrong side) Using A, knit 1 row.

(Right side) Begin double seed stitch; work even until the piece measures 54" (137cm) from the beginning (corner block measures 9" [23cm]), ending with (wrong-side) row 2 or 4 of the pattern.

Bind off all stitches loosely in pattern.

CENTER PANELS

Lower Border

Using C, cast on 98 stitches.

(Wrong side) Knit 1 row.

Begin Patten

(Right side) K4 (keep in garter stitch throughout), place a marker; beginning row 1, work garter stitch basket weave across the center 90 stitches; place a marker, k4 (keep in garter stitch throughout).

Continue in this way, keeping 4 stitches each side in garter stitch and center stitches in pattern, slipping the markers as you come to them, until the piece measures 9" (23cm) from the beginning, ending with a wrong-side row.

Fasten off C; join E.

Cable Leaf Block

(Right side) Using E, k1, increase 1 (k1-f/b) in the next stitch, k47, increase 1 in the next stitch—51 stitches; place the remaining 49 stitches on a holder for vine leaf block, turn.

(Wrong side) Working on these 51 stitches only, purl 1 row.

Begin Pattern

(Right side) [K1, p2—edge stitches], place a marker; beginning row 1, work cable leaf pattern over the center 45 stitches; place a marker, [p2, k1—edge stitches].

(Wrong side) [K3], slip the marker; work pattern across the center stitches; slip the marker, [k3].

Continue in this way, working cable leaf pattern on the center 45 stitches and edge stitches as indicated, until the piece measures 18" (45.5cm) from the lower border, ending with a wrong-side row.

Fasten off E.

Place the stitches on the holder.

Vine Leaf Block

Place 49 stitches from the first holder onto the needle; join D, ready to work a right-side row.

(Right side) Knit, increasing 5 stitches evenly across—54 stitches.

Begin Pattern

(Wrong side) K1 (keep in garter stitch throughout); beginning row 1, work 26-stitch multiple of vine leaf pattern twice over the center 52 stitches; k1 (keep in garter stitch throughout).

Continue in this way, keeping 1 stitch each side in garter stitch, until the piece measures 18" (45.5cm) from the lower border, ending with a wrong-side row.

Fasten off D.

Place the stitches on a holder.

Join Blocks

Leaving the stitches on the holders, sew the center seams between the cable leaf and vine leaf blocks.

Encased Leaves Block

Place 51 stitches from the cable leaf block onto the needle; join F, ready to work a right-side row.

(Right side) Knit, increasing 3 stitches evenly across—54 stitches.

Begin Pattern

(Wrong side) K8 (keep in reverse stockinette stitch throughout), place a marker; beginning row 1, work encased leaves panel across the center 38 stitches, referring to the leaf insert for stitches 24–28 (if working from the chart); place a marker, k8 (keep in reverse stockinette stitch throughout).

Continue in this way, working stitches on each side of the markers in reverse stockinette stitch and pattern on center stitches until the piece measures 18" (45.5cm) from the cable leaf block, ending with a wrong-side row.

Fasten off F.

Place the stitches on a holder.

Bobble Leaves Block

Place 54 stitches from the vine leaf block onto the needle; join G, ready to work a right-side row.

(Right side) Work 2 rows in stockinette stitch (knit 1 row, purl 1 row), ending with a wrong-side row.

Begin Pattern

(Right side) *P3 (keep in reverse stockinette stitch throughout), place a marker; beginning row 1, work bobble leaves panel across the next 21 stitches; place a marker, p3 (keep in reverse stockinette stitch throughout); repeat from * once.

Continue in this way, working stitches on each side of the markers and center 6 stitches in reverse stockinette stitch, and in pattern on the remaining stitches, referring to the leaf insert as indicated (if working from the chart), until piece measures 18" (45.5cm) from the vine leaf block, ending with a wrong-side row.

Fasten off G.

Place the stitches on the holder.

Join Blocks

Leaving the stitches on the holders, sew the center seams between the encased leaves block and the bobble leaves block.

Upper Border

Place the stitches from both holders on the needle; join C, ready to work a right-side row—108 stitches.

(Right side) Knit 2 rows, decreasing 10 stitches evenly across the first row—98 stitches.

Begin Patten

(Right side) K4 (keep in garter stitch throughout), place a marker; beginning row 1, work garter stitch basket weave across the center 90 stitches; place a marker, k4 (keep in garter stitch throughout).

Continue in this way, keeping 4 stitches each side in garter stitch and center stitches in pattern, slipping the markers as you come to them, until the piece measures 9" (23cm) from the beginning of the border, ending with a wrong-side row.

Bind off all stitches loosely.

LEAF EDGING

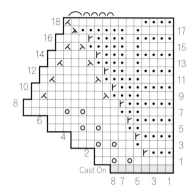

☐	Knit on right side, purl on wrong side
☒ (•)	Purl on wrong side, knit on right side
☒ (o)	Yo
☒ (ꓑ)	Increase 1
☒	Ssk on right side, p2tog on wrong side
☒	K2tog
☒	P2tog
☒	Psso

LEAF EDGING (MAKE 2 PIECES)

Using B, cast on 8 stitches.

Row 1 (right side) K5, yo, k1, yo, k2.

Row 2 P6, knit into the front and the back of the next stitch (increase 1), k3.

Row 3 K4, p1, k2, yo, k1, yo, k3.

Row 4 P8, increase 1, k4.

Row 5 K4, p2, k3, yo, k1, yo, k4.

Row 6 P10, increase 1, k5.

Row 7 K4, p3, k4, yo, k1, yo, k5.

Row 8 P12, increase 1, k6.

Row 9 K4, p4, ssk, k7, k2tog, k1.

Row 10 P10, increase 1, k7.

Row 11 K4, p5, ssk, k5, k2tog, k1.

Row 12 P8, increase 1, k2, p1, k5.

Row 13 K4, p1, k1, p4, ssk, k3, k2tog, k1.

Row 14 P6, increase 1, k3, p1, k5.

Row 15 K4, p1, k1, p5, ssk, k1, k2tog, k1.

Row 16 P4, increase 1, k4, p1, k5.

Row 17 K4, p1, k1, p6, [slip 1, k2tog, psso], k1.

Row 18 P2tog, bind off the next 5 stitches *using p2tog stitch to bind off the first stitch*, p3, k4.

Continue in this way, repeating rows 1–18, until the piece measures the same length as one short end of the throw, ending with (wrong-side) row 18 of the pattern.

Bind off the remaining stitches.

FINISHING

Block the pieces to the measurements by steaming lightly, being careful not to flatten the texture.

Using the yarn needle, weave in all ends.

ASSEMBLY

Sew the side panels to the center panel, matching the corner blocks of the side panels to the upper and lower borders (see the diagram). Sew the leaf edging to the short ends.

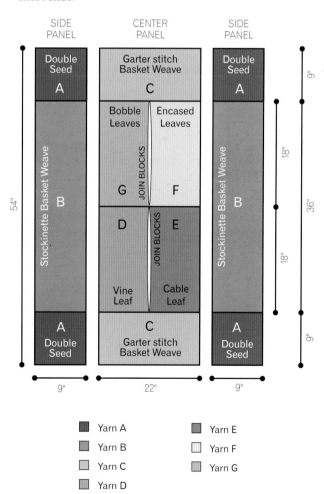

◼	Yarn A
◼	Yarn B
◻	Yarn C
◻	Yarn D
◼	Yarn E
◻	Yarn F
◻	Yarn G

Lake District Throw

DESIGNED BY GITTA SCHRADE

Tweed yarn adds a special dimension that takes this throw from an ordinary, uninspired piece of knitting to an extraordinary work of art. The four corners frame the throw with applied leaf shapes.

To make this an easier project, color-photocopy the charts. Then tape them together to create the whole picture. Keeping track of rows is essential for this project, so mark off the rows as you work them. Also, choose smaller sections to work in duplicate stitch rather than working all colors in the intarsia method.

EXPERIENCED

KNITTED MEASUREMENTS

38½" x 50½" (98cm x 128.5cm)

MATERIALS

5 skeins Tahki Yarns Donegal Tweed (100% pure new wool, 3½ oz [100g], 183 yd [167m]) in #867 taupe (MC) and 1 skein each in #866 gray (A), #893 rust (B), #846 yellow (C), #847 red (D), #874 maroon (E), #818 pink (F), #849 light purple (G), #894 dark olive (H), #879 olive (J), #892 green (K), #815 dark blue (L), #843 medium blue (M), #809 teal (N), #839 bronze (P), and #890 black (Q) 4 medium

Size 8 (5mm) needles, or size needed to obtain gauge

Size E-4 (3.5mm) crochet hook

Yarn needle

Bobbins (optional)

GAUGE

18 stitches and 24 rows = 4" (10cm) in stockinette stitch

TAKE TIME TO CHECK GAUGE.

ABBREVIATIONS AND TERMS

psso (pass slip stitch over knit stitch)

PATTERN STITCHES

Chain

Wrap the yarn around the crochet hook (yarn over), and draw it through the loop on the hook to form the first chain.

Seed Stitch

Row 1 (right side) *Knit 1, purl 1; repeat from * to end.
Row 2 (wrong side) Purl the knit stitches and knit the purl stitches. Repeat rows 1 and 2 for seed stitch.

Single Crochet

Insert the hook in the stitch, yarn over and pull up a loop, yarn over and draw through both loops on the hook.

Stockinette Stitch

Knit on the right side, purl on the wrong side.

Notes: Work from the chart in stockinette stitch, intarsia method, using a separate ball of yarn for each section. Do not strand yarn across the wrong side of the work.

The chart is separated into four sections, each 81 stitches wide by 144 rows high (see the diagram).

If desired, small areas of color may be worked in the background color for that section, then duplicate-stitched after the throw is completed. Veins on leaves and stems can also be worked in back stitch, using the colors suggested on the chart, for a more textured look, especially if using the throw as a wall hanging.

Many of the leaves for the various flowers overlap on the throw, creating large areas of green; to help you distinguish the individual leaves, the sections have been outlined on the charts. After working the throw, you may want to use back stitch in one or more of the leaf colors to outline the individual leaves and set them apart from one another; center veins in the leaves can also be worked with back stitch, rather than duplicate stitch, if desired.

THROW

Using MC, cast on 162 stitches.

Begin working from the chart.

Work 288 rows.

Bind off all stitches in pattern.

FINISHING

Using the yarn needle, weave in all ends, taking extra care at color changes to tighten up any loose stitches.

Complete any areas in duplicate stitch or back stitch that were worked in background colors.

Block the piece to the measurements.

Crochet Edging

Work 3 stitches in each corner stitch of every round.

Join each round with a slip stitch in the first stitch.

When changing colors, join the new color in the last stitch of the round; then join the round with a slip stitch in the first stitch and continue with the new color for the next round.

With the right side facing, using the crochet hook and D, join the yarn with a slip stitch to the lower-right-hand corner.

Round 1 Chain 1, work 1 row of slip stitch evenly around, working 3 slip stitches in each corner stitch, join with a slip stitch in the first stitch.

Round 2 Chain 2, single crochet in each slip stitch around, working 3 single crochet in each corner, join.

Round 3 Chain 2, single crochet in each single crochet around, working 3 single crochet in each corner, join.

Fasten off D; join F (see notes above).

Rounds 4–5 Using F, work as for round 3.

Fasten off F; join P.

Round 6 Using P, work as for round 3.

Fasten off P; join Q.

Round 7 Using Q, work as for round 3.

Fasten off.

Using the yarn needle, weave in the ends. Block the edging, if necessary.

LEAF A (MAKE 1 LEAF EACH USING B, J, K, AND N)

Cast on 5 stitches.

Row 1 (right side) K2, yo, k1, yo, k2—7 stitches.

Row 2 and all wrong-side rows Purl.

Row 3 K3, yo, k1, yo, k3—9 stitches.

Row 5 K4, yo, k1, yo, k4—11 stitches.

Row 7 K5, yo, k1, yo, k5—13 stitches.

Row 9 K6, yo, k1, yo, k6—15 stitches.

Row 11 K7, yo, k1, yo, k7—17 stitches.

Row 13 Ssk, k13, k2tog—15 stitches remain.

Row 15 Ssk, k11, k2tog—13 stitches remain.

Row 17 Ssk, k9, k2tog—11 stitches remain.

Row 19 Ssk, k7, k2tog—9 stitches remain.

Row 21 Ssk, k5, k2tog—7 stitches remain.

Row 23 Ssk, k3, k2tog—5 stitches remain.

Row 25 Ssk, k1, k2tog—3 stitches remain.

Row 27 Knit.

Row 28 Purl.

Row 29 Slip 1, k2tog, psso.

Fasten off.

LEAF B (MAKE 1 LEAF EACH USING H, J, AND N)

Cast on 5 stitches.

Row 1 (right side) K2, yo, k1, yo, k2—7 stitches.

Row 2 and all wrong-side rows Purl.

Row 3 K3, yo, k1, yo, k3—9 stitches.

Row 5 K4, yo, k1, yo, k4—11 stitches.

Row 7 K5, yo, k1, yo, k5—13 stitches.

Row 11 Ssk, k9, k2tog—11 stitches remain.

Row 13 Ssk, k7, k2tog—9 stitches remain.

Row 15 Ssk, k5, k2tog—7 stitches remain.

Row 17 Ssk, k3, k2tog—5 stitches remain.

Row 19 Ssk, k1, k2tog—3 stitches remain.

Row 20 Slip 1, k2tog, psso.

Fasten off.

LEAF C (MAKE 1 LEAF EACH USING J AND P; MAKE 2 LEAVES USING B)

Cast on 5 stitches.

Row 1 and all right-side rows Work as for Leaf B.

Row 2 and all wrong-side rows Knit.

LEAF D (MAKE 1 LEAF EACH USING K AND P)

Cast on 5 stitches.

Row 1 (right side) K2, yo, k1, yo, k2—7 stitches.

Rows 2, 4, 6, and 8 Knit.

Row 3 K3, yo, k1, yo, k3—9 stitches.

Row 5 K4, yo, k1, yo, k4—11 stitches.

Row 7 Ssk, k9—10 stitches remain.

Row 9 Ssk, k8—9 stitches remain.

Row 10 Ssk, k7—8 stitches remain.

Row 11 Ssk, k6—7 stitches remain.

Row 12 Knit.

Row 13 Ssk, k5—6 stitches remain.

Row 14 Ssk, k4—5 stitches remain.

Row 15 Ssk, k3—4 stitches remain.

Row 16 Knit.

Row 17 Ssk, k2—3 stitches remain.

Rows 18–20 Knit.

Row 21 Slip 1, k2tog, psso.

Fasten off.

LEAF E (MAKE 1 LEAF USING H; MAKE 2 LEAVES USING K)

Cast on 5 stitches.

Row 1 (right side) K2, yo, k1, yo, k2—7 stitches.

Row 2 and all wrong-side rows Purl.

Row 3 K3, yo, k1, yo, k3—9 stitches.

Row 5 K4, yo, k1, yo, k4—11 stitches.

Rows 7, 11, 15, 19, and 23 Knit.

Row 9 Ssk, k7, k2tog—9 stitches remain.

Row 13 Ssk, k5, k2tog—7 stitches remain.

Row 17 Ssk, k3, k2tog—5 stitches remain.

Row 21 Ssk, k1, k2tog—3 stitches remain.

Row 25 Slip 1, k2tog, psso.

Fasten off.

FINISHING

Block the leaves.

Attach 4 leaves to each corner, using the diagram as a guide.

CHART DIAGRAM/LEAF PLACEMENT

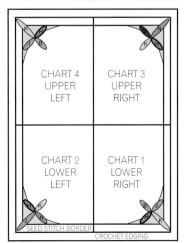

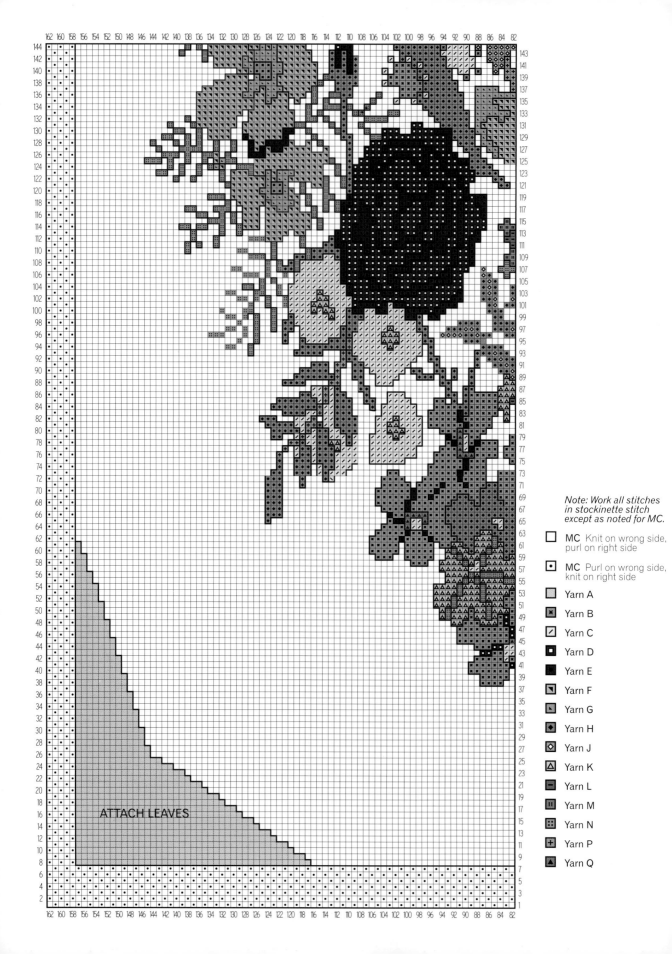

Note: Work all stitches in stockinette stitch except as noted for MC.

☐ MC Knit on wrong side, purl on right side

⊡ MC Purl on wrong side, knit on right side

▦ Yarn A

✳ Yarn B

◪ Yarn C

◱ Yarn D

◼ Yarn E

◣ Yarn F

◩ Yarn G

◆ Yarn H

◈ Yarn J

△ Yarn K

⊟ Yarn L

⫲ Yarn M

⊞ Yarn N

⊞ Yarn P

▲ Yarn Q

ATTACH LEAVES

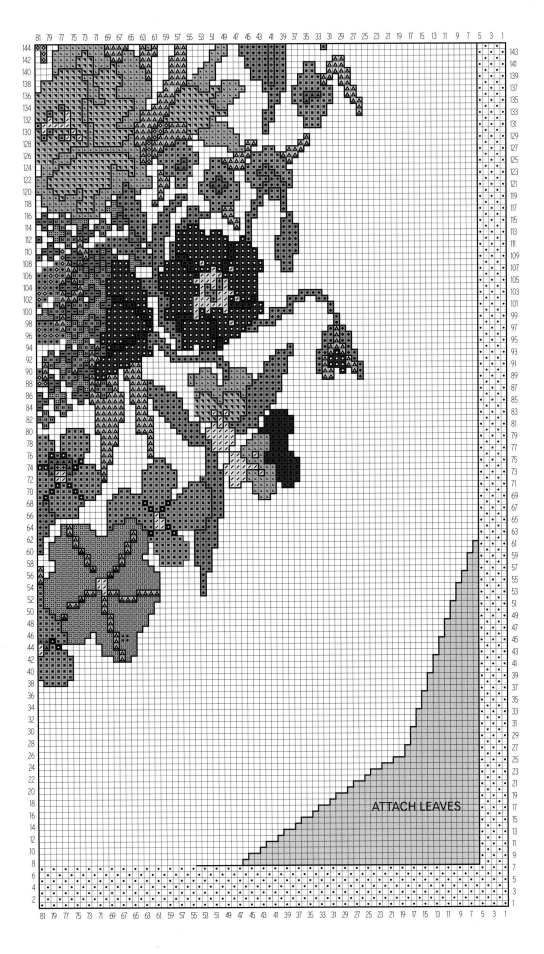

ATTACH LEAVES

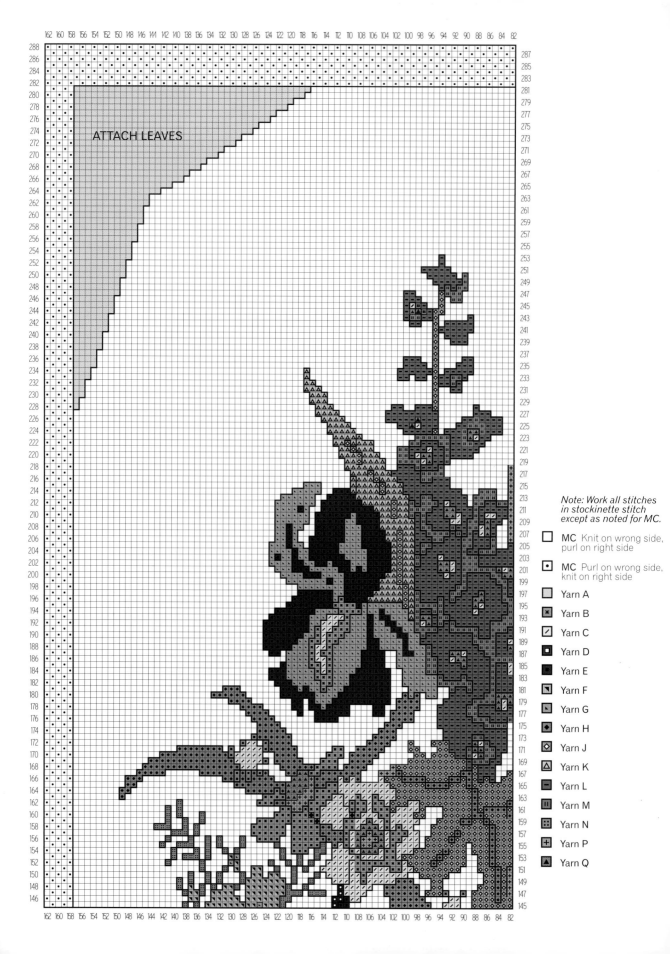

ATTACH LEAVES

Note: Work all stitches
in stockinette stitch
except as noted for MC.

☐ MC Knit on wrong side,
purl on right side

⊡ MC Purl on wrong side,
knit on right side

▦ Yarn A

✳ Yarn B

◪ Yarn C

⊡ Yarn D

◼ Yarn E

◥ Yarn F

◣ Yarn G

◈ Yarn H

◇ Yarn J

△ Yarn K

▬ Yarn L

▥ Yarn M

▦ Yarn N

✚ Yarn P

▲ Yarn Q

ATTACH LEAVES

Resources

All the projects in this book call for yarns by Tahki Stacy Charles. Knitters can purchase Tahki yarns online at www.tahkistacycharles.com or from fine yarn stores across the country.

Stores that carry Tahki Stacy Charles yarns:

CALIFORNIA

Enchanged Unicorn
415 Tennessee Street
Suites E and F
Redlands, CA 92373
909-792-2046
www.enchantedunicorn.com

Knitting Arts
14554 Big Basin Way
Saratoga, CA 95070
408-867-5010
www.goknit.com

Nine Rubies LLC
28 E. Third Avenue, #100
San Mateo, CA 94401
650-685-6205
www.ninerubies.com

COLORADO

Shuttles, Spindles & Skeins, Inc.
635 South Broadway, Unit E
Boulder, CO 80305
303-494-1071
www. shuttlesspindlesandskeins.com

CONNECTICUT

Sit 'n' Knit
33 LaSalle Road
West Hartford, CT 06107
860-232-9276
http://sit-n-knit.com

INDIANA

Mass Avenue Knit Shop
862 Virginia Avenue
Indianapolis, IN 46203
317-638-1833
www. massaveknitshoponline.com

Stitches & Scones Inc.
120 North Union Street
Westfield, IN 46074
317-896-4411
www.stichesnscones.com

MARYLAND

Woolworks
6117 Falls Road
Baltimore, MD 21209
410-377-2060
www.woolworksbaltimore.com

MASSACHUSETTS

Creative Warehouse
220 Reservoir Street
Needham, MA 02494
781-444-9341
www. elissascreativewarehouse.com

A Good Yarn
4 Station Street
Brookline Village, MA 02447
617-731-4900
www.agoodyarn.biz

Webs
75 Service Center Road
Northampton, MA 01060
413-584-2225
www.yarn.com

Wild and Woolly Enterprises
7A Meriam Street
Lexington, MA 02420
781-861-7717

The Wool Basket
19 Depot Street
Duxbury, MA 02331
781-861-7717

MICHIGAN

Ewe Nique Yarns Inc.
9864 East Grand River
Suite 160
Brighton, MI 48116
810-229-5579
www.ewe-niqueyarnsinc.com

NEW HAMPSHIRE

Patternworks (mail order)
PO Box 1618
Center Harbor, NH 03226
603-253-8148
www.patternworks.com

NEW JERSEY

Wooly Monmouth
9 Monmouth Street
Red Bank, NJ 07701
732-224-9276
www.woolymonmouth.com

Yarnware (mail order)
627 Eagle Rock Avenue
West Orange, NJ 07052
877-369-9276
www.yarnware.com

NEW MEXICO

Village Wools
5916 Anaheim Avenue NE
Albuquerque, NM 87113
505-883-2919
www.villagewools.com

NEW YORK

Flying Fingers
15 Main Street
Tarrytown, NY 10591
877-359-4648
www.flyingfingers.com

The Yarn Company
2274 Broadway
New York, NY 10024
212-787-7878
www.theyarnco.com

NEVADA

Jimmy Beans Wool
5000 Smith Ridge Drive, #A11
Reno, NV 89502
877-532-3891
www.jimmybeanswool.com

OREGON

Soft Horizons Fibre
412 East Thirteenth Avenue
Eugene, OR 97401
541-343-0651

VIRGINIA

Needle Lady
114 East Main Street
Charlottesville, VA 22902
434-296-4625
www.needlelady.com

WASHINGTON

A Grand Yarn
1314 South Grand Boulevard
Spokane, WA 99202
509-455-8213
www.agrandyarn.com

Main Street Yarn
15217 Main Street
Mill Creek, WA 98012
425-337-9606

Seattle Yarn Gallery
5633 California Avenue SW
Seattle, WA 98136
206-935-2010
www.seattleyarn.com

Weaving Works
4717 Brooklyn Avenue NE
Seattle, WA 98105
888-524-1221
www.weavingworks.com

WISCONSIN

Lakeside Fibers
402 West Lakeside Street
Madison, WI 53715
608-257-2999
www.lakesidefibers.com

CANADA

The Old Mill Knitting Company
1334 Osprey Drive Unit 1
Ancaster, Ontario L9G 4V5
Canada
905-648-3483
www. oldmillknitting.com/retail.htm

Yarn Substitution Guide

The following guide, organized by yarn weight, lists all the Tahki Stacy Charles yarns used in this book and offers suggestions for substitution. If you're not sure whether a particular yarn can be used as a substitute, make a swatch first to determine whether the gauges match. The fabric should be similar in texture, drape, and appearance. Since the amount per skein varies, be sure to base your substitution on total yardage rather than the number of skeins.

MEDIUM (WORSTED, AFGHAN, ARAN) 〔4〕 MEDIUM

127 Print: Cascade 220 Quatro by Cascade Yarns; Encore Colorspun Worsted by Plymouth Yarn; Equinox Stripe by Nashua Handknits; and Inca Print by Classic Elite.

Donegal Tweed: Harrisville Highlands by Harrisville Designs; Lamb's Pride Worsted by Brown Sheep Company; Creative Focus Worsted by Nashua Knits; Silkroad Aran Tweed by Jo Sharp; Lopi Lite by Reynolds/JCA; and Skye Tweed by Classic Elite.

New Tweed: Summer Tweed by Rowan; Cotton Jeans by Rowan; Silkroad DK Tweed by Jo Sharp; and Whiskey by Reynolds/JCA.

Shannon Tweed: Paint Box by Knit One, Crochet Too; Kid Classic by Rowan; Encore Colorspun Worsted by Plymouth; Boku by Plymouth Yarn; and Keltic by Berroco.

Torino: 1824 Wool by Mission Falls; Julia by Nashua Handknits; Pure Merino by Berroco; Aurora 8 by Karabella Yarns.

BULKY (CHUNKY, CRAFT, RUG) 〔5〕 BULKY

Soho Tweed: Wool/Silk by Himalaya Yarns; Lopi by Renolds/JCA; Lamb's Pride Bulky by Brown Sheep Company; and Shetland Chunky by Patons.

Yarn Weight Chart

YARN WEIGHT SYMBOL & CATEGORY NAME	OTHER NAMES OF YARNS	KNIT GAUGE RANGE IN STOCKINETTE STITCH TO 4 INCHES (10CM)	RECOMMENDED NEEDLE SIZE RANGE
〔4〕 MEDIUM	worsted, afghan, aran	16 – 20 stitches	U.S. 7 – 9 (4.5 – 5.5 mm)
〔5〕 BULKY	chunky, craft, rug	12 – 15 stitches	U.S. 9 – 11 (5.5 – 8 mm)

Index

BOSTON PUBLIC LIBRARY

3 9999 06117 554 1